Simply Sensational

Rubber Stamping

Simply Sensational

Rubber Stamping

Jane Pinder

David and Charles

This book is dedicated to my husband Noel,
daughter Sam and son Mike. Without their love
and support I could not have completed this
book. And to my Mum and Dad, brother Richard
and sister Fryn, just thanks for being there.

A DAVID & CHARLES BOOK
Copyright © David & Charles Limited 2006

David & Charles is an F+W Publications Inc. company
4700 East Galbraith Road
Cincinnati, OH 45236

First published in the UK in 2006

Text and project designs copyright © Jane Pinder 2006

Jane Pinder has asserted her right to be identified as
author of this work in accordance with the Copyright,
Designs and Patents Act, 1988.

A catalogue record for this book is available from
the British Library.

ISBN-13: 978-0-7153-2328-1 paperback
ISBN-10: 0-7153-2328-8 paperback

Printed in China by SNP Leefung
for David & Charles
Brunel House   Newton Abbot   Devon

Commissioning Editor Vivienne Wells
Editor Jennifer Proverbs
Desk Editor Bethany Dymond
Art Editor Sarah Underhill
Production Controller Kelly Smith
Project Editor Juliet Bracken
Photography Karl Adamson and Ginette Chapman

Visit our website at www.davidandcharles.co.uk

David & Charles books are available from all good
bookshops; alternatively you can contact our Orderline
on 0870 9908222 or write to us at FREEPOST EX2 110,
D&C Direct, Newton Abbot, TQ12 4ZZ (no stamp
required UK only); US customers call 800-289-0963
and Canadian customers call 800-840-5220.

Contents

Introduction

One of the best things about rubber stamping is that anyone can do it, since all the drawing has been done for you. All you have to do is let your imagination loose, play with colour and soon you will be creating the most amazing designs.

I often hear stampers say that they lack the ability, or time, to think of what to make. This is where the book can help you. It is packed with design ideas to try, and I hope it will also inspire you to take stamping further.

Rubber stamping has been around for many years and is as popular now as it has ever been. Why? In the fast-paced world we live in, it is so good to sit down quietly and make a unique card or gift for someone by hand. The pleasure it gives both you, the creator, and the person who receives it, cannot be measured. It is also a wonderful way of relaxing and a lot of fun. You will be amazed how the time goes while you sit at your work table.

When you first start stamping, all the different products can seem rather daunting, but you don't need to buy everything all at once. Start off with two or three stamps and a couple of dye-based ink pads. Then progress on to embossing and to other forms of ink pad

and colour. Once you have mastered those, you can move on to plenty more techniques, some of which will involve other products.

If, like many stampers, you already have a knowledge of other crafts, you may well find that they overlap with stamping. You can use many of the same tools and equipment, for example beads, threads, fibres and wire. All will make wonderful embellishments for your work.

Above all, enjoy your stamping, experiment with your own ideas and don't let anyone tell you that you cannot do something. Try it – you might just invent a new technique in the process!

How to use this book

If you are new to stamping, go to the guide to basic tools overleaf. This describes the tools needed at the beginning and the techniques they are used for. After that it is straight into the projects and down to work. Some are ideal for beginners, others will provide more of a challenge. Whatever your level of stamping, work your way through the book and you will be surprised at what you can achieve.

It can be so frustrating when a stamp you've seen on a project is no longer produced, so I have used the Artifacts range of stamps throughout the book. We can guarantee these will be available for a good time to come because my husband and I produce the Artifacts stamps. See page 125 for suppliers.

Basic Tools

As with most crafts, you will need some basic tools for rubber stamping. As your knowledge grows, your tool kit will probably expand, too. In this chapter you will find the basic items that are necessary right from the start. You may already have some of them and will need to buy others. However, each item will get used over and over again, not just for the projects in this book, but throughout your stamping career.

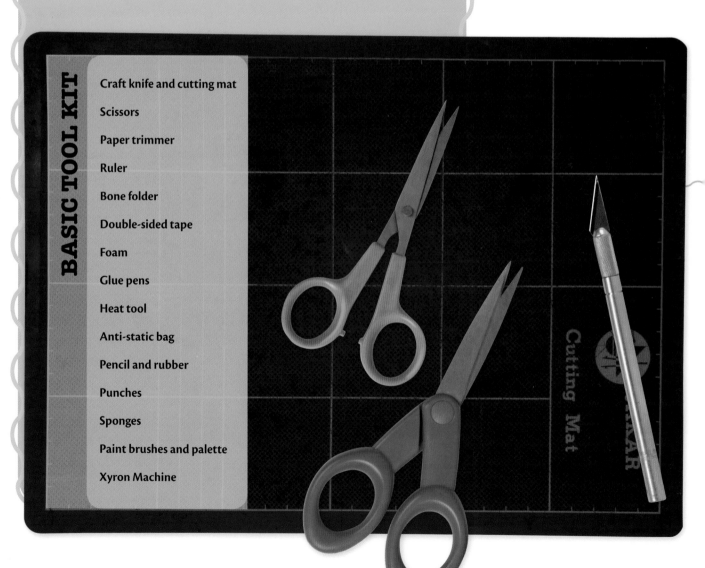

BASIC TOOL KIT

Craft knife and cutting mat

Scissors

Paper trimmer

Ruler

Bone folder

Double-sided tape

Foam

Glue pens

Heat tool

Anti-static bag

Pencil and rubber

Punches

Sponges

Paint brushes and palette

Xyron Machine

RULER

You will find two types of ruler useful: a transparent ruler for measuring and positioning markers, and a metal ruler for using with a craft knife. Ideally, the metal ruler should have a finger indentation along its length to protect your fingers from the blade of the knife.

SCISSORS

After a craft knife, the next most important thing you need is a sharp pair of scissors. Two or three pairs would be really useful. We all have our favourite pair, so find some that suit you and keep them safe.

FOAM

Double-sided sticky foam is just what you need for adding depth to a layered piece of work. This is available on a roll and in large, medium, small, or mini, pre-cut squares.

BONE FOLDER

Once the card is cut to size, the next tool needed is a bone folder. This will help you crease and fold card neatly. It can also be used for scoring paper and for smoothing creases. Most are now made of resin, although you sometimes find wooden or bone ones.

CRAFT KNIFE AND CUTTING MAT

One of the most important tools is a good, sharp craft knife and a cutting mat to go with it. They will ensure the card or paper stays flat while you cut intricate designs from it. It takes a little practice to get used to using a craft knife, but it is worth persevering. Check that the blade is always sharp and replace it regularly, because card and paper will dull it. An A4 cutting mat is the most useful size. And never use a heat tool on the mat as it will distort it.

PAPER TRIMMER

An A4 paper trimmer is a good investment, especially if you make cards from an A4 sheet of card. There are several different ones available and those with replaceable blades are best.

DOUBLE-SIDED TAPE

This tape is invaluable for adding layers to a design as it is both quick and clean to use. It comes in various sizes: you will find the very narrow and 1cm (½in) wide tape most useful.

ANTI-STATIC BAG

This is a useful tool when embossing onto a dark coloured card. If you wipe it over the surface before you start embossing, the bag will help prevent the powder from sticking to unwanted areas of the card and spoiling the design.

GLUE PENS

This is an invaluable tool for applying glue without getting your fingers sticky. One type of glue pen – the Changing Glue Pen can be used both as a permanent adhesive and as a repositionable glue, if you apply it then leave to dry before attaching an item.

HEAT TOOL

This tool is designed mainly for use with embossing powders and shrink plastic (see pages 18 and 20), although they can also be used to dry inks. Several styles are available and they are all meant for craft use. Choose one that feels comfortable to you. My preference is for the white tool as it is both light and fairly quiet. They do produce an intense heat so work surfaces must be protected with a wooden board before you start work on a project.

PENCIL AND RUBBER

A simple lead pencil is vital for marking your card, ideally a 2H as this can be easily rubbed out. Keep your pencil well sharpened and use a good, soft plastic rubber which rubs out marks cleanly.

> **TIP**
> *Remember to sharpen your pencil before you put it away. Then, when you come to use it next time, it is all ready to go.*

More Creative Options

Other useful tools that can be added later to extend your creativity.

PUNCHES

There are hundreds of different size, shaped paper punches you can use to create decorative patterns on cards or make pretty embellishments with. The first two punches I would recommend buying are a ⅛in and a ¹⁄₁₆in single hole punch. These tools are simple, but very useful. You can use them to attach brads and eyelets, or to make holes through which fibres and ribbons can be threaded.

SPONGES

A sponge is useful for applying colour from an ink pad. You can create a different effect by varying the type of sponge texture. For example, a natural sponge gives a lovely open pattern, while others create a smooth look. If you don't like getting your fingers too dirty, try a Sponge Dauber.

PAINT BRUSHES AND PALETTE

It is a good idea to have two or three different size brushes for different jobs. For example, you will need a good quality brush both to apply colour and to remove specks of embossing powder. A paint palette is useful for mixing colours taken from ink pads or re-inker bottles. You can also use it as a place to put small items, such as beads or eyelets, while you are working.

XYRON MACHINE

This handy machine will apply an even coating of adhesive to the back of card, ribbon, punched shapes and many other materials. It is very easy to use, and helps you keep your fingers clean. It is available in various sizes and you can buy a replacement cartridge when you need to. Some machines also take cartridges for adding a magnet to the back of your work and for laminating items.

There will be more tools that you pick up as you go on, but with these in your kit, you will be well on the way!

Paper and Card

Paper is a vital ingredient in card making, and there is a huge variety to choose from – including plain, pearlescent, mirror, patterned, vellum – and many more. Go for the best quality papers you can find. Paper is sold in A4 sheets, in scrapbooking sizes – 12 x 12in or 8 x 8in pieces – or in pads of various sizes. It may say it is for scrapbooking, but there's no reason why you can't use it for stamping. You will soon start to build up a collection of papers and card. Remember to keep all the off-cuts because they're sure to be useful for other projects later.

COLOUR

Colour can make or break your stamped work, so choose carefully. Some colours will drain your work, while others will bring the shades to life. Don't forget that this applies to the inks you use as well as the the layers of card and paper. Experiment with dark colours, too. Look for the ink pads you can buy that are suitable for stamping on dark colours, such as StazOn opaque white.

PATTERNS

Patterned or background papers are ideal for adding layers to your work. When selecting one from the huge choice available, make sure that the pattern works with your stamped design without overpowering the image. Some patterned papers can be stamped or tinted with inks to create an aged look.

MULBERRY PAPER

Mulberry paper is fantastic and can be used to create layers on all your works of art. What's more, you can stamp on mulberry paper as well. It has a lovely texture and can be given a frayed edge by applying a line of water to it and gently pulling it apart. When dry, you will have a pretty feathery edge. These papers can also be used for covering books and boxes, ready for applying your stamped images to.

TEXTURE AND FINISH

There are many different textures and handmade papers that will add a tactile value to your work, as well as providing colour. Mirror and shiny card will create another look, when used in moderation. Many unlikely surfaces can be stamped on, such as wrapping paper, wallpaper and paper serviettes, and they are ideal for use in collage work.

PAPER VELLUM

This is a favourite among stampers. It comes in many different colours and shades, as patterns or plains, even with an embossed texture. It can be stamped on or used as it is, and it makes a wonderful artistic background. Many inks can be used on vellum, making it very versatile. Try stamping on it, or turning it over and applying colour on the reverse for a wonderful soft effect.

> ### TIP
> *Always choose your colour combinations with care. To help with this, collect paint sample strips from a DIY store and use them to experiment with different colours.*

Stamping Basics

Here I will show you how to find your way round the different types of stamps and the multitude of ink pads you can buy, and what they are used for. Once you have these essential ingredients for stamping, what do you do with them? Read on to find out just some of the ways you can use your supplies and how to store and look after your stamps.

Rubber stamps

There are so many stamp designs to choose from, it's hard to know where to start. The easiest answer is to choose a design that pleases you – there are sure to be many that you like, but that is only part of the answer.

Stamps can be wood mounted, foam mounted or un-mounted. Clear stamps are not rubber stamps as they are made of polymer, but they are used in exactly the same way as their rubber cousins. Whichever type you opt for, the quality and use is the same.

Rubber stamps fall into two main categories:

Flat, solid stamps

The image is usually less defined on this type of stamp, and all the colour is applied before stamping using marker pens.

Outline stamps

These stamps produce just that, an outline, to which you can add colour after it has been stamped onto card or paper.

Some stamps are both flat and outline stamps.

Inks

You now need to consider the type of ink you are going to use. With so many different ink pads around, it can be a bit of a minefield. Here is an idea of what the different ink pads can be used for.

When choosing an ink pad, consider the surface you will be stamping on – for example, whether it's glossy, if you are using leather or vellum, shrink plastic or wood – all these need careful thought.

Dye-based ink pads

Dye-based pads are quick drying, translucent inks that are water based and usually come on a hard felt pad. The colours tend to be non-permanent, although there are a few exceptions. They may be used on most cards, vellums and papers, and the image will be brighter on glossy card. These pads are available in solid colours or as multi-coloured rainbow pads (above).

Pigment ink pads

These pads are opaque and usually come on a foam pad. The ink itself is thicker than dye ink and they are available in many colours and colour combinations. Some colours are available as pearlescent, metallic or chalk finish ink pads. The original pigment ink pads were slow drying, making them suitable for embossing as well as stamping (see page 18), but you can now buy faster drying pigment ink pads. They can be used on most surfaces, but it is worth checking the labels first

to make sure. The newer, faster drying pads are ideal for shrink plastic, acetate, leather, clay, glass and foil, to name but a few surfaces (see bottom of page).

VersaMark ink pads also come under this category. They are used to create a lovely watermark effect on card by taking the colour of the card down a tone. They can also be used as an embossing ink pad.

Embossing ink pads

As the name suggests, these pads are used in combination with embossing powders and a heat tool. They are slow drying inks which give you enough time to add embossing powder before they dry. The pads are available in a clear or a tinted ink. You can buy embossing pens filled with the same ink, which are used in the same way as the ink pads (see top right of page).

Specialist inks

Other specialist inks such as Fabric and Crafter's ink pads are available for use on wood, fabric, unglazed ceramics such as Style Stones and shrink plastic. They usually need to be heat set, using a heat tool (see page 18), for the ink to be permanent. Permanent ink pads work well on semi-porous and non-porous surfaces such as glass, acrylic, metal foil and acetate.

New ink pads for stamping are appearing all the time, and are fun to try. Read the labels to see if they are dye-based, pigment, or one of the other types, and you will not go wrong.

Looking after stamps and ink pads

If you look after your stamps and ink pads, they will reward you with many years of use. Never clean wood-mounted stamps under running water and don't immerse them in water. To clean them, use a tray with damp kitchen paper in it. Pat the stamp on this to remove the ink, then pat it on some dry kitchen paper. A soft toothbrush can help to remove the ink from any fine detail. An alcohol-free baby wipe may also be used to remove the ink residue.

Ink pads do run out of ink, and can be re-inked using the small bottles of ink you can buy. Make sure you use the correct re-inker for the particular ink pad. Simply add ink evenly over the surface of the pad and use a piece of thick card to drag the ink across the surface. Continue doing this until all the ink has been soaked up. Do not apply the whole bottle of ink!

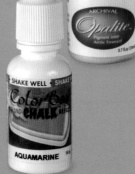

Storing your stamps

Here are a few suggestions to help prolong the life of your stamps and keep them organised.

Always make sure your stamps are clean before you put them away. There's nothing worse than going to use a stamp, only to find you forgot to clean it last time.

Store your stamps away from direct sunlight, away from a window. Extremes of temperature can affect the rubber.

When you buy a stamp, stamp it in a plain notebook and note the manufacturer, stamp name and code number and where you bought it. Then you shouldn't buy the same stamp twice. It's also a good idea to 'log' your pens and ink pads at the back of the book. Over time it will become a piece of art in its own right.

How to Stamp

You can start making beautiful impressions with your stamps straight away. Begin with an ink pad and then move on to trying brush markers and embossing.

Using an ink pad

Using an ink pad is easy. All you do is pat the stamp on the surface of the ink pad and then press it firmly onto card or paper. Press over the whole of the stamp on the back using an even pressure and make sure you do not rock it as this will give a blurred image. Lift the stamp off while holding the card down on the work surface and it will leave behind a wonderful impression.

Using brush marker pens

If you wish to have more control over where the colour goes on the stamp, you need to apply it with brush marker pens. There is a wide choice of colours available, and the possible colour combinations are endless. You can also place the colours where you want them to go, rather than relying on the ink pad to put ink all over the stamp.

1 Start with the stamp, rubber side up, and use the large tip on the brush marker to apply colour directly to the surface. If you are using more than one colour pen on your stamp, use the lightest colour pen first, then graduate down to the darkest colour. This will avoid contaminating your pens.

2 Next you will need to 'huff' on the inked surface, to make the moisture in your breath re-activate the ink so that it makes a good impression.

3 Now stamp the image onto the paper or card, applying an even pressure as before. You can also use watercolour pencils, chalks or another medium.

More Techniques

Embossing and shrink plastic are two techniques you can use with stamping to create fabulous designs for cards and many other projects.

Embossing

The next technique to try is embossing. This creates a raised image using an embossing ink pad, some embossing powder and a heat tool, and is just like magic! You can emboss many different surfaces including card, foil, wood, paper and heat-proof acetate.

Originally, embossing powder was only available in gold, silver and copper but now there are hundreds of different colours to choose from. The powders also come in a metallic, pearlescent, glittered, coloured or clear finish. The metallic and coloured powders tend to be opaque, the clear ones are transparent, pearlescent powders are semi-transparent and the glittered ones can be any of these.

Where to start

Most stampers begin with gold or silver embossing powder which have to be used with an embossing ink pad. You can use an opaque powder with either a clear or tinted embossing ink pad. A VersaMark ink pad is also suitable. A coloured pigment ink pad can be used, especially if you choose a colour to match the embossing powder.

When using a transparent or semi-transparent powder, you need to think about the colour of pigment ink pad you use, because this colour will be visible through the embossing.

How to emboss

Start by inking up your stamp with one of the embossing ink pads, then stamp the image onto your card. At this stage, if you used the tinted pad you will just be able to see the image.

Place the stamped card onto a sheet of scrap paper, then sprinkle your chosen embossing powder over the wet image. Tap off the excess powder onto the sheet of scrap paper. This can then be funnelled back into the container for use at a future date.

Now put the card onto a wooden board and use the heat tool to heat the image. Hold the tool about 2.5cm (1in) away from the image and, as the powder melts, move the nozzle to the next area. As soon as the image has gone from a powdery finish to a shiny finish, stop heating and turn off the heat tool. If you overheat the powder it will look oily and seem to sink into the card instead of looking shiny and standing proud. As soon as it is cool enough to touch, you can add colour using Le Plume pens, coloured pencils or watercolours.

How to Add Colour

When you need to add colour to an embossed or a stamped image you have no end of choice. Here are some of the different forms of colour you can try. It's a good idea to experiment with as many as you can to find your favourite!

Watercolour effect

For a softer look, use the watercolour technique. This allows you to build up layers of colour and to blend colours together to create some subtle shading. Scribble some colour from the pens onto a palette and use a wet paint brush to apply it to your work. When using this technique, you must stamp the image with a permanent ink pad or the lines will bleed.

Watercolour pencils (shown above) can be used in a similar way, either direct from the pencil or by taking the colour from the tip of the pencil with a wet paint brush. Either way, the colours can again be blended on the card.

Le Plume pens

The easiest way is to use the Le Plume type pens which come in a huge range of colours. They can be used direct from the pens to give strong colours or with a watercolour technique.

Chalks

Decorating chalks also give a lovely soft finish and are ideal for delicate designs. Chalks can be applied with small balls of cotton wool or a cotton bud. If you wish to add more depth to the design, a chalk enhancer is available. Chalks come in palettes of 9 or 24 colours in several colour ranges and they can be used with any type of ink pad.

Shrink Plastic

I have now covered the basic techniques in stamping. There are, of course, many more ways to use stamps, and you will encounter some of them in the projects in the book. However, there is one technique that needs explaining here and that is how to use shrink plastic.

Shrink plastic is a plastic material that has been heated and then stretched in two directions to form a thin sheet, and is a wonderful surface on which to stamp. It is used by first stamping an image onto it, then cutting it out and heating it again to make it return to its original size and thickness. An image stamped onto shrink plastic will usually shrink to about 45 per cent of the original size after being heated.

Types of shrink plastic

You can buy different types of shrink plastic, each of which has its own quality.

Clear shrink plastic

This type is ideal for a see-through technique in which colour is applied to the back of the piece. When the piece is turned over to the right side the colour becomes vibrant and it gives a certain depth to the item. This type is also useful if you want to create a glass-like piece to add to your card.

Translucent shrink plastic

This has a lovely soft look and is useful when large areas of the image are left free of colour.

Coloured shrink plastic

Use white shrink plastic if you want the colours to be crisp. It is amazing how very detailed stamp images will shrink down perfectly. Black shrink plastic gives a dramatic finish and can be used with coloured pencils, metallic pens and inks to create rich results.

How to use shrink plastic

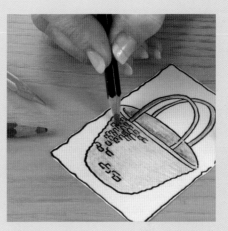

1 Sand your chosen type of shrink plastic lightly (you can also buy pre-sanded shrink plastic). Use a sanding block to sand it in a cross hatch pattern. This will give the surface a key and ensure that the ink will stay in place.

2 Stamp your image onto the shrink plastic. Use a suitable ink pad for this, such as Brilliance, Crafter's or StazOn (see page 15). All of these will become permanent during the heat shrinking process.

3 Carefully add colour to the image with pencils or chalks. Be careful, however, because the ink will still be wet. You will need to cut out the image at this stage, before shrinking. Take great care not to smudge the design. You also need to punch any holes now because, once shrunk, it will be too thick to do this.

4 Place the piece on an old wooden board and heat it with a heat tool. You may need to gently hold it in place using a wooden kebab stick. As the heat is applied, the plastic will start to move and twist around. Don't panic – this is perfectly normal and part of the shrinking process. Continue heating the piece – you may need to turn it over and apply heat from the other side.

5 Once it has stopped contorting, switch off the heat tool and place the wooden side of a stamp on top of the plastic to help keep it flat while it cools. But remember not to press the wood down as this may cause the warm plastic to become mis-shapen.

> ## HELP, I'M SHRINKING
>
> *If the shrink plastic curls up and sticks to itself during the shrinking process, stop heating and allow it to cool a little.*
>
> *Then gently pull it apart – you will hear a small snap as this happens. Then continue heating to finish the shrinking.*

Start Stamping!

COOL

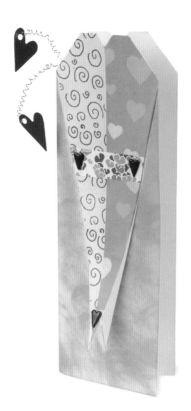

With all my Heart

We often look for a card so we can send our love to someone. This pretty heart-shaped design is ideal for many such occasions, from Valentine's Day to a last-minute birthday. It is made using easy stamping and masking techniques, and finished off with punched red hearts suspended from coiled wire. The result is a stylish, elegant card which is perfect for sending a greeting from the heart.

TECHNIQUE FOCUS
Gold wire is wonderful for embellishing a card. It is easy to create a coiled effect by wrapping the wire around a cocktail stick.

You will need

- ❖ Double-sided Stars and Swirls Texture stamp
- ❖ Cream card – A4 sheet scored and folded lengthways
- ❖ Pink heart scrapbooking paper
- ❖ Small pink and red hearts scrapbooking paper
- ❖ Scraps of red card
- ❖ Heart template (see page 120)
- ❖ Fluid Chalk ink pad – pink pastel

- ❖ Red embossing powder
- ❖ Medium folk heart punch
- ❖ Small hole punch
- ❖ Silver wire
- ❖ Three red heart brads
- ❖ Needle tool
- ❖ Sponge
- ❖ Cocktail stick
- ❖ Large Post-it notes
- ❖ Basic tool kit (see page 8)

See page 126 for product details

1 Place the heart template over the folded card and line it up with the top. Draw round lightly with a pencil. Cut round the top on both pieces to create a shaped edge.

2 Open the card out and, with the craft knife, cut from the point of the heart to about half way up, on both sides. Curl up the bottom of the heart slightly, so that it sticks out slightly from the card.

3 Stick Post-it notes along the outside line of the heart shape, to act as a mask. Stamp swirls across the heart with embossing ink, making sure you cover the left hand side completely. Heat emboss with red embossing powder.

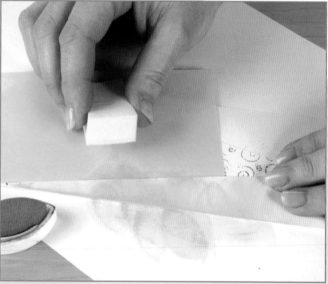

4 Move the Post-it notes to the other side of the pencil line so that they now cover up the heart. Apply pink pastel chalk ink with a sponge, to create a colour wash all around the heart shape.

TIP

Keep odd lengths of leftover wire. You'll be surprised how often you can use them for making embellishments.

5   Flip the template over and draw round it on the back of the pink hearts paper. Cut out the shape. Using a ruler, draw a line down the centre from the point to the top. Cut along it to form a half heart shape. Stick this to the right hand side of the heart on the card with a glue stick.

6   Cut a strip of the small red and pink hearts scrapbooking paper and stick this across the middle of the heart. Add the heart brads – two in the middle over the strip of heart paper and one at the point of the heart.

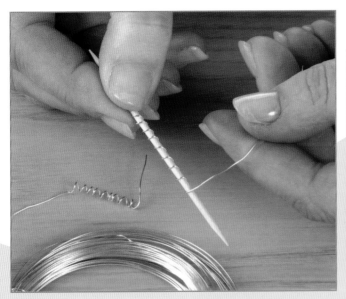

7   Cut two, 8cm (3.5in) lengths of silver wire. Wrap each piece tightly around a cocktail stick to make two springs. Leave a short straight piece at one end of each spring.

8   Punch two hearts out of the red card scraps. Punch a small hole on one side of each heart and thread the coiled end of a spring through each one.

To complete the card: Attach the springs at the straight end to the inside of the card at the top with strong glue. Wait until the glue dries before closing the card.

TIP
Before stamping, wipe the card with an anti-static puff to prevent excess powder sticking to it and spoiling the image.

Precious Baby

What could be nicer than creating a card to welcome a new baby? At such a special time new parents will receive plenty of cards, and a handmade one is sure to stand out from the rest. Soft shades of blue, pink or a pastel lemon are ideal for this design. A glazing technique is used on the centre panel. This involves heating a layer of clear embossing powder spread on top and gives a smooth, glossy finish. There is also a simple resist technique to try. The decorative edges on the card were made with a border punch.

You will need

❖ Baby Rattle stamp
❖ Collage Dotty Wisp stamp
❖ Precious Baby stamp
❖ White folded card – 12cm (4¾in) square
❖ Turquoise card – 12 x 10cm (4¾ x 4in)
❖ Silver card – 5cm (2in) square
❖ Vellum – 12 x 9cm (4¾ x 3½in)

❖ Extra white card
❖ Marvy Le Plume pen – light blue
❖ Versamark ink pad
❖ Fluid Chalk ink pads – ice blue and Prussian blue
❖ Clear embossing powder
❖ Border punch
❖ Basic tool kit (see page 8)

See page 126 for product details

TECHNIQUE FOCUS

Here's a technique you won't be able to resist. Clear emboss your design, then sponge or brayer coloured ink over the top and watch your images emerge.

1 Cut a 4cm (2¾in) wide strip from the right edge of the front of the folded card. Ink up the rattle and the dotty wisp stamps with the VersaMark ink pad and stamp them onto the remaining card front. Sprinkle the wet images with clear embossing powder, tap off the excess powder and heat with a heat tool (see page 18).

2 Using a sponge wedge, pick up some colour from the ice blue chalk ink pad and apply it over the embossed images. Use a clean sponge to apply a little Prussian blue ink over the top. The clear embossing will resist the ink, allowing the images to show through the colours.

3 Pick out the ribbon details on each embossed rattle by colouring it with the pale blue pen.

4 Use the same blue pen to apply colour directly to the rattle stamp. Stamp this image onto white card and trim it to measure 4cm (2¾in) square. Then dab the stamped square with the VersaMark ink pad and sprinkle it with clear embossing powder. Tap off the excess powder, and heat with a heat tool to give an attractive glazed finish.

5 Mount this piece onto turquoise card using double-sided tape, then trim it to leave a 5mm border all round. Mount this in turn onto silver card and trim this to leave a narrow border all round.

6 On the inside back of the card, stamp the Precious
Baby image using a combination of the two blue ink
pads. Start by applying the ice blue ink all over the stamp,
then add touches of the Prussian blue ink.

7 Once the inks are dry, place a piece of scrap paper
along the left hand edge of the wording panel, to leave
the words exposed. Dab the VersaMark ink pad over the
words, then sprinkle the wet image with clear embossing
powder. Tap off the excess powder and heat as before.

TIP

*When applying more than one colour to a stamp or a
stamped image, start with the lightest colour ink. This will
prevent your pens and ink pads being contaminated.*

8 Take the vellum and turquoise card and use the
border punch down one long side of each piece.

9 Use double-sided tape to attach the vellum strip to
the back of the card front so that the decorated edge is
showing. Stick the strip of turquoise card behind the vellum with
its decorative edge showing beyond the vellum one.

To complete the card: Use sticky foam pads to attach the square
rattle panel to the centre front of the card.

Spirit of Adventure

Make this unusual card for a keen explorer. It was created using a lovely multi-image collage stamp and coloured in with soft, natural, earthy shades. This gives a wonderful antique look that is perfect for this stamp. The individual images are highlighted by a simple 3D layering technique which adds further interest and depth. The card is finished off with the words 'daring' and 'brave' taken from another collage stamp showing behind a torn edge.

You will need

- ❖ Spirit of Adventure stamp
- ❖ Describe Him stamp
- ❖ Cream card – 10.5 x 15cm (4 x 6in) when folded
- ❖ Extra cream card
- ❖ Tan card
- ❖ Gold paper
- ❖ Mulberry or other handmade paper
- ❖ VersaFine ink pad – vintage sepia

- ❖ VersaMark ink pad
- ❖ Clear embossing powder
- ❖ Coloured pencils
- ❖ Marvy Le Plume pen – dark brown
- ❖ Fibres – shades of brown
- ❖ Silicone glue or sticky foam pads
- ❖ Basic tool kit (see page 8)

See page 126 for product details

TECHNIQUE FOCUS

You don't always have to stamp the whole image. You can create some exciting effects using only parts of an image, or by going over the edge of the card.

1 Stamp the Spirit of Adventure image three times onto the spare cream card using the vintage sepia ink pad. Leave a border around each one so you can cut each one out.

2 Cut off one of the images and trim to leave a 5mm (¼in) border at the sides and bottom and a slightly wider border at the top. Trim off the two top corners to form a tag shape. Separate the remaining two images.

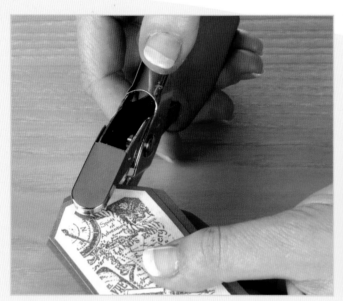

3 Using double-sided tape, mount the tag onto gold paper and trim to leave a narrow border all round. Mount this in turn onto the tan card and trim it again. Punch a hole in the centre top through all three layers.

4 Use coloured pencils to shade the mounted image, keeping to soft tones throughout. Select individual elements of the design to highlight with 3D layering, such as the luggage and compass. Shade these in on the other two stamped images and cut out round them.

5   Dab VersaMark ink onto these cut out pieces, sprinkle them with clear embossing powder, tap off the excess and heat them with a heat tool to give a glazed finish (see page 18).

6   Use silicone glue or sticky foam pads to fix the first layer of these extra pieces to the tag. When dry, add the second layer to create a 3D look. Thread the fibres through the hole in the top of the tag and tie them in a knot.

7   Tear off about one third from the opening edge of the main cream card. Then tear a piece of mulberry paper cut to the same size as the card front, down the right hand edge. Ink up the words 'daring' and 'brave' on the Describe Him stamp with the dark brown pen and stamp them onto the mulberry paper.

To complete the card: Stick the mulberry paper to the inside front of the card and the tag at an angle on the card front.

TIP
Protect your work surface with a layer of scrap paper before you start stamping, especially when the image runs over the edge of the card.

Perfect Pyramid

What do you do when you have found just the right gift for someone, but it's a difficult shape to wrap? Easy: you make a box to fit it! This wonderful pyramid-shaped box is perfect for awkward shapes and is fun to make. You can use your stamping skills to decorate it, and add such embellishments as a moulded tag, fibres, sequins and flower buttons. The result is a stunning gift box that will be treasured as much as the gift it conceals.

You will need

- ❖ Orchid Border stamp
- ❖ Time in Motion stamp
- ❖ Ancient Script stamp
- ❖ Small oval tag Art Mould
- ❖ Lilac card – A4 sheet
- ❖ Brilliance pigment ink pads
  – peacock, Victorian violet
- ❖ Fluid Chalk ink pads
  – lavender, aquamarine
- ❖ Purple Metallic Mesh
  – four, 2.5cm (1in) squares
- ❖ Magic Mesh for stencil
- ❖ Delight paper clay
- ❖ Four large round sequins
- ❖ Four flower buttons
- ❖ Purple eyelash fibre
- ❖ Silver glitter glue
- ❖ ⅛in hole punch
- ❖ Super glue gel
- ❖ Stylus tool
- ❖ Basic tool kit
  (see page 8)

See page 126 for product details

TECHNIQUE FOCUS
A box is an ideal project for using up leftover materials and embellishments that can be coloured to match the design.

1 Tear off a piece of the clay and press it into the mould. Start in the middle and work towards the edges to eliminate any air bubbles. Leave it in the mould (or carefully remove it), then set aside for 24 hours to dry.

2 Trace the pyramid template on page 118 onto the lilac card. Cut it out and score along the fold lines using the stylus tool. Crease the folds, making them all valley folds, except for the four short lines around the edge. These should be mountain folds.

3 Stick a strip of Magic Mesh randomly on one of the box sides. Sponge some aquamarine and some lavender chalk ink over the mesh and around the edges. Peel off the mesh and move it to the next box side and repeat. Do this on the other two sides and then on the base.

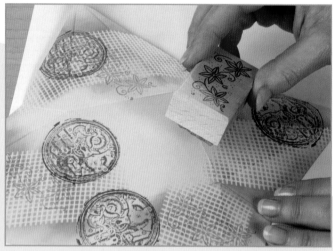

4 Ink up the Time in Motion stamp with the Victorian violet ink pad and stamp it randomly, once on each box side, four times in all. Then ink up the Orchid Border stamp with the aquamarine chalk ink pad and stamp it once on each box side and also on the base panel.

TIP

Valley folds are made so that the card folds upwards. Mountain folds are the opposite: where the card folds downwards.

5 Ink up the Ancient Script stamp with the peacock pigment ink pad and stamp it once on each box side as well. You can overlap this stamp on to the base.

TIP

When using spray adhesive, place the item in a box and spray into the box. This prevents the spray from going all over your work surface.

6 Apply spray adhesive to each piece of purple mesh and stick one onto each side of the box. To help the mesh to stick, press the back of a stamp down on each piece as you position it on the box. Then attach a large sequin onto each mesh square. Super glue works well for this and will ensure that the mesh stays in place. Add a flower button to each sequin, again with super glue.

7 Punch a hole in the top of each box side with the hole punch. Thread a length of eyelash fibre through the first hole and then fold up the box, so that all the points are together. Thread the fibres in and out through the other holes and pull them gently to keep the box shut.

8 Punch through the hole in the top of the oval moulded tag. Sponge some aquamarine and some lavender chalk ink onto both the back and front of the tag.

9 Stamp the Orchid Border image onto the coloured moulded tag using the lavender chalk ink pad, then stick on a small flower button with super glue. Thread one end of the fibre through the hole in the tag.

To complete the pyramid: Add a spot of silver glitter glue in the centre of each flower button. Leave to dry before concealing your gift inside the box.

TIP

Magic Mesh is a sticky-backed grid ribbon that can be punched, cut, and sponged through to embellish a card.

Perfect Pyramid

bags and boxes

Here are some more sensational gift bags and boxes you can create using easy stamping techniques that will transform your gifts into something special. They're made from the templates on page 118 and details of the products used are on page 126.

PEN BAG

This bag will add the perfect finishing touch to a gift for a man. It was stamped with a mixture of brown inks and gold embossing powder, using the following stamps: Pen Nibs, Time in Motion, Postscript and Ancient Script (see page 126). At the top of the bag is a panel of gold printed vellum attached with two small brads. This was also edged with a gold Krylon pen. Two holes were punched in the front and back of the bag and threaded with string for the handles. Each handle was secured with a knot and a small tag was attached to one of the ends of string before it was secured. This was cut from card, sponged and embossed with a greeting.

COOL SURFING

This pillow box was decorated with shrink plastic t-shirt and shorts motifs and stamped with the Palm Leaves image before being shrunk with a heat tool (see page 18). The cut out box shape was sponged with a blue ink pad, then overstamped with more palm trees, surfing and cool images (see page 126) using dark blue ink, then embossed with clear embossing powder. The clothes were mounted on mulberry paper. Two holes were punched in either side of the box to thread fibres through for fastening it. These are kept in place by a bead. The box is assembled by folding in the curved lines scored earlier.

THANK YOU PILLOW BOX

This simple design for a thank you gift is made using the pillow box template on page 122. It was stamped with the swirl side of the Double-sided Stars and Swirls Texture stamp using an ink to match the card. Other small swirls were gold embossed randomly over the top. The assembled box was decorated with the Thank You image, gold embossed onto card edged with a gold Krylon pen and attached with a gold paper clip to some gold card layered with corrugated card. An organza ribbon bow adds the finishing touch.

BEAUTIFUL BUTTERFLIES

This delicate design was made using the bag template on page 119 and stamped with the Geometric stamp on the front and back. Several butterfly images were silver embossed on to a contrasting shade of card and vellum, cut into squares of varying sizes and attached to the bag front and back. Two ribbon handles were glued in place on both sides at the top of the bag.

HEARTS AND FLOWERS

This bag was made from a pre-cut shape which had all the fold lines pre-punched, and stamped with a selection of images in shades of ink that tone with the bag. Some of these were silver embossed as a contrast. To finish, a small embellishment mounted on organza ribbon was added and the handle decorated with a selection of pretty fibres and a matching feather.

Star Qualities

This stunning card is the ideal way to let your man know how much you care. It is made using a descriptive stamp and some fun techniques. The rich burgundy background card looks gorgeous dusted with pearl effect powders. Layered on top are three smaller squares, gold embossed using the same stamp. In opposite corners are two stars punched from metal and beautifully coloured using Alcohol Inks. It's the perfect design for revealing your feelings in a subtle and elegant way.

You will need

- ❖ Describe Him stamp
- ❖ Off-white card blank
  – 12cm (4¾in) square
- ❖ Dark blue card
  – 9.5cm (3¾in) square
- ❖ Burgundy card
  – 8.5cm (3½in) square
- ❖ VersaMark ink pad or clear embossing pad
- ❖ Gold embossing powder
- ❖ Metal sheet – silver
- ❖ Length of wire
- ❖ Alcohol Inks – meadow, cranberry and lettuce
- ❖ Applicator tool for Alcohol Inks
- ❖ PearlEx pigment powders – gold and copper
- ❖ Soft applicator brush
- ❖ Folk star lever paper punch or other small punch of your choice
- ❖ Basic tool kit (see page 8)

See page 126 for product details

TECHNIQUE FOCUS

The effect will be different each time you use Alcohol Inks because the inks blend and merge together to form a unique colour.

1 Ink the Describe Him stamp with the VersaMark ink pad and stamp it close to the right-hand edge of the burgundy square. Repeat to create an all-over design.

2 Load a tiny amount of pigment powder onto the applicator brush and dust over the image until the desired effect is achieved. Use the brush to dust off any excess powder. Use sticky foam pads to mount the patterned burgundy square onto the dark blue square.

TIP
Avoid overloading your brush when using powder pigments. Only pick up a small amount each time for this technique.

3 Using embossing ink, stamp the Describe Him stamp onto another piece of dark blue card. Sprinkle the image with gold embossing powder and heat (see page 18). Trim close to the embossed image to form a long rectangle, and cut into three equal pieces. Mount one embossed square just in from the top left-hand corner of the burgundy square and another in the bottom right-hand corner, using double-sided tape. Reserve the third square.

4 Use the Alcohol Inks to colour a piece of silver metal. Do this by dabbing each colour in turn onto the applicator tool and then using this to dab the colour onto the metal. When the coloured metal is dry, use the paper punch to punch out two or more stars.

5 Take a piece of wire and form a spiral at one end and a larger spiral at the other end. Loop one spiral over the bottom left-hand corner of the burgundy card square and the other spiral over the top right-hand corner.

6 Attach sticky foam pads to the back of both the metal stars and the last embossed square. Use these pads to secure the wire to the card by fixing the embossed square in the centre of the card and one of the stars over the spiral in each corner.

To complete the card: Use double-sided tape to attach the completed panel onto the front of the card.

TIP

For a stronger bond, attach the stars with silicon glue instead of sticky foam pads.

Origami Blue

Here's a wonderful idea for a card to make for the man in your life! It was created using both sides of a pretty double patterned stamp and an easy paper folding technique. The folded papers are stuck together in a circle and mounted on turquoise and blue pearlescent card. Although this card was designed with men in mind, a simple change of colour would make it suitable for the ladies as well.

You will need

❖ Double-sided Stars and Swirls Texture stamp
❖ Pearlescent card – deep blue, 20 x 21cm (8 x 17in), and 6cm (2½in) square
❖ Pearlescent card – turquoise, two, 7cm (2¾in) squares
❖ White paper
❖ Embossing ink pad

❖ Fluid Chalk ink pad – Prussian blue
❖ Clear embossing powder
❖ Silver embossing powder
❖ 5cm (2in) square paper punch
❖ Sponge wedge
❖ Basic tool kit (see page 8)

See page 126 for product details

TECHNIQUE FOCUS
Simple paper folding or origami gives a lovely effect and turns a card into a 3D work of art.

1 Fold the pearlescent card in half to form a 10 x 21cm (4 x 8½in) card. Tear two strips of scrap paper and temporarily fix to the front of the card, leaving an exposed blue strip of about 5cm (2in) running down the centre from top to bottom.

2 Ink the star side of the texture stamp with embossing ink and stamp it over the exposed part of the card. Re-ink and stamp over the entire exposed area. Remove the paper masks and sprinkle the wet images with clear embossing powder, tap off the excess and heat (see page 18).

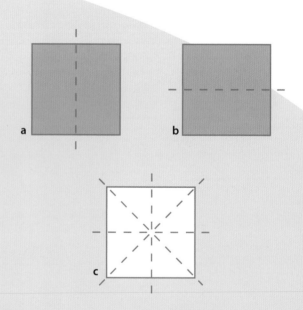

3 Using the embossing ink pad, stamp the star side of the texture stamp onto white paper and emboss with silver powder. Repeat three more times. Stamp and emboss with silver powder using the swirl side of the stamp four times as well. Punch out four, 5cm (2in) squares in each design. Pick up some Prussian blue ink with the sponge wedge and apply lightly to the swirl embossed squares.

4 When dry, fold each square as follows:
a Fold in half vertically, pattern side inwards, crease and open out flat.
b Fold in half horizontally, pattern side inwards, crease and open out flat.
c Fold in half diagonally both ways, pattern side outwards, crease and open out flat. You now have four folds in total.

5 Hold the corners on one of the diagonal folds and move together into the centre. The other folds will help in this process and you will end up with a triangle that is a quarter of the size of the original square. Press it all flat.

6 Hold the folded triangle with the point towards you and pick up the left-hand flap. When vertical, open the flap and press it flat. Fold each piece in this way and attach double-sided tape to the back.

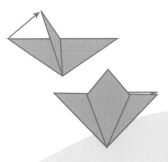

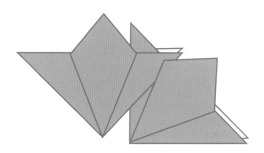

7 Assemble the pieces, alternating a blue with a white one. Place the single edge of one piece between the double edge of the previous one. Continue round until you have used every piece.

TIP

Try placing the origami piece towards the top of the card. Then you will have space underneath to add a layered greeting.

8 Stick the Prussian blue card square to a turquoise square with double-sided tape and trim round it to leave a narrow border. Attach the assembled origami in the centre with double-sided tape.

To complete the card: Stick the second turquoise square to the front of the main card with double-sided tape 5cm (2in) from the top of the card. Use the same tape to attach the mounted origami diagonally on top.

Star Delight

Starbooks make a beautiful showcase for favourite pictures or stamped images. They contain eight sections or pages that are stuck together. They have a front and a back cover and, when opened out completely, form a star shape. A star book can tell a story from beginning to end, and gives the perfect opportunity for using different stamping techniques. It's an exciting format to try if you are thinking of making a miniature scrapbook for an important occasion or to dedicate to someone special.

You will need

❖ Cream card – eight, 10 x 8.5cm (4 x 3½in) pieces
❖ Dark blue card – eight, 13 x 8.5cm (5¼ x 3½in) pieces
❖ Sand coloured card – eight, 15 x 8.5cm (6 x 3½in) pieces
❖ Thick mount board – two, 9cm (3½in) squares
❖ Co-ordinating scrapbooking or decorative paper – one sheet
❖ Cord or string – about 60cm (24in)
❖ Krylon gold pen

For the inside pages:
❖ Selection of stamps and dye-based ink pads, embossing powders and embossing ink pad
❖ Found objects such as shells or small stones
❖ Stickers to suit your theme
❖ Embellishments such as buttons, coiled wire, bubble stickers, beads or brads
❖ Basic tool kit (see page 8)

See page 126 for product details

Decorating the pages of the book

There are many ways you can decorate the pages of your book and it's fun to experiment. On one page I used a blue dye-based ink pad with a geometric stamp and added some domed stickers, a piece of torn paper and a circle of coloured shrink plastic. The other side is gold embossed with an ancient script image and has a small shrink plastic frame displaying a picture of some beach pebbles. Another page was stamped in terracotta with a collage splatter image and also has a shell sticker. I stamped a sea life image onto shrink plastic, punched a hole in the top and heated it. Colour was then applied direct from a blue Brilliance ink pad and beads attached through the hole with a piece of gold wire.

1 Cut the 24 card pieces for the pages with a paper trimmer. Fold each one in half across the width and crease it with a bone folder. Draw around the edges of each one with the gold pen. Hold each page in the centre and place the pen nib on the edge. Push the card slightly into the pen nib and then run it firmly all the way round. Then decorate the pages using a mixture of stamping and embossing, stickers and embellishments.

2 When you have finished decorating the pages, put them all face down and stick a piece of double-sided tape along the two short sides of each one. Leave the tape backing on for now.

3 Slot each decorated cream card into a dark blue piece of card, ready for sticking. Remove the backing on the first cream edge and line it up with the edge of the blue piece. Stick the two pieces together firmly. Do the same on the other side, and repeat with all the cream and blue pieces.

4 Stick strips of double-sided tape on the two short edges of each blue card piece and match them up in the same way onto the sand card. Stick the eight sets of pages together by attaching tape to the outer edges on each one; remove the tape backing and press together.

6 Cut the paper diagonally across each corner about 2mm (⅛in) away from the board corner. Apply glue to the triangle of paper showing and fold the corner over onto the mount board. Fold opposite corners together to ensure the paper is pulled tight. Cut another square of the paper to fit over the folded down edges on the inside to form a lining (inset). Stick this in place with glue or double-sided tape. Repeat on the other cover.

5 Place the two pieces of mount board on the back of some decorative paper. Cut round the board leaving a 5cm (2in) border around each one. Apply glue to each piece of mount board and stick them onto the paper. These will form the book covers.

8 Apply glue or tape to the back of the first and last pages. Hold the pages shut, remove the tape backing and attach the front cover to the back of the first page. Keep the book shut and attach the back cover in the same way.

To complete the card: Open it all the way out when completely dry and tie the string together to form the star-shaped book.

7 Stick the string across the back of the front cover, and onto the back of the back cover, leaving a 2.5cm (1in) gap between the two covers for the spine, and equal ends hanging from each side.

Pretty Wrapping

Did you know you can create your own special wrapping paper in minutes using easy stamping techniques? It's a wonderful way to dress up a gift, especially if you also make a tag to match, as I did here. I chose a white pearlescent paper which has a sheen that's ideal for a festive wrapping paper. I gold embossed two different star stamps and a Christmas tree image randomly across it. If you tie the parcel with matching organza ribbon your gift will look fabulous.

You will need

For the gift wrap:
- ❖ Starry Christmas Tree stamp
- ❖ Swirls and Star stamp
- ❖ Small Star stamp
- ❖ White pearlescent paper – one sheet
- ❖ Fluid Chalk ink pad – lipstick red
- ❖ Distress ink pads – peeled paint and fired brick
- ❖ Embossing ink pad

- ❖ Gold embossing powder
- ❖ Clear sparkle embossing powder
- ❖ Gold glitter glue

For the tag:
- ❖ Triple Tag stamp
- ❖ Green textured card
- ❖ Red card
- ❖ Red mixed fibres
- ❖ Basic tool kit (see page 8)

See page 126 for product details

TECHNIQUE FOCUS
You can create your own gift wrap from many types of paper, even ordinary brown paper.

For the Gift Wrap ...

1 Stamp the Starry Christmas Tree, and Swirls and Star images all over the paper using the embossing ink pad. Sprinkle the images with gold embossing powder, tap off the excess powder and heat with a heat tool (see page 18).

2 Apply the Small Stars stamp using the peeled paint and fired brick ink pads between the star and tree images. Sprinkle on clear sparkle embossing powder and heat.

3 Fill in the small stars on the tree image with gold glitter glue and allow them to dry.

4 Sponge lipstick red chalk and peeled paint ink all over the sheet.

To complete the gift wrap: Simply allow to dry, and you will be ready to wrap your gift!

TIP
Change the colour of the pearlescent paper and the stamps used to create birthday wrapping paper. Use images of bells and horseshoes and you have wedding paper.

Pretty Wrapping

For the Tag ...

1 Apply embossing ink to the largest tag outline on the Triple Tag stamp and stamp it onto the green card. Gold emboss the image (see page 18) and cut out the tag shape.

2 Punch a hole in the top then randomly stamp and gold emboss the Small Star image on the tag.

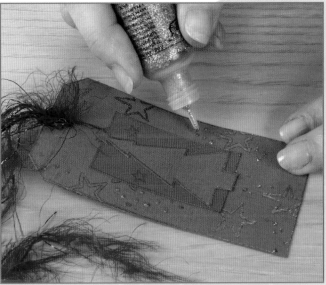

3 Stamp the Christmas tree stamp once on to red card and once on to green card, with embossing ink and gold emboss both images. Cut out the tree from the green card and cut around the outside frame on the red image.

4 Stick the green tree on to the red panel and stick the whole panel on to the tag.

To complete the tag: Add some dots of gold glitter glue to the tag and thread some fibres through the hole. Then attach this pretty tag to your parcel to give it a perfect finish.

christmas creations

Christmas is an excellent time to show off your creative skills. Here are some sensational ideas for stamped festive designs to make for your family and friends. See page 126 for details of the stamps used.

SHIMMERING SNOWFLAKES

A pearlescent white embossing powder was used to randomly emboss the Snowflake stamp over a textured card on this lovely festive design. It was then sponged with ink from a blue ink pad. More snowflakes were made by silver embossing the same image onto pearlescent blue card and cutting them out with a round punch. These were attached to the card with sticky foam pads. Finally, a small hole was punched in the top left hand corner to attach some fancy blue fibres.

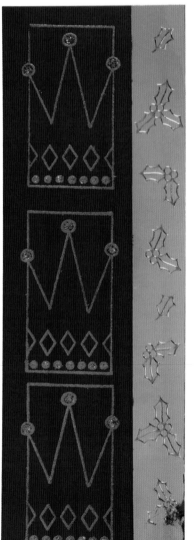

THREE CROWNS

This stylish card has three Christmas Crown images gold embossed down its left side. It is made from pearlescent blue card and has a strip of gold mirror card down the right edge decorated with small gold holly shaped peel offs.

STARS AND TRIANGLES

This striking triangular card is cut from dark green pearlescent card. The front is randomly embossed with the Small Star stamp using gold embossing powder (see page 18). A couple of the stars are coloured in with copper glitter glue. The motif is made in the same way as the gift tag on page 57 with the Starry Christmas Tree stamp – by gold embossing it onto red and green card, and cutting out the whole image from the red card and just the tree from the green. The tree was attached to the red image with sticky foam pads.

RED AND GOLD COLLAGE

A deep shade of red card makes an ideal background for this collage design. It was gold embossed with the star side of the Double-sided Stars and Swirls Texture stamp and has a torn piece of toning patterned paper in two opposite corners. The torn edges were run across an embossing ink pad, dipped in gold embossing powder and heated before the papers were taped in place. In the centre is another Swirls and Star image gold embossed on to gold mirror card, cut out and attached with sticky foam pads.

SHRUNK TO FIT

This slender card is decorated with a shrink plastic Christmas tree motif mounted on gold metal and mulberry paper. The tree shape was stamped on shrink plastic before heating using a gold Brilliance ink pad and filled in with star motifs from the same double-sided texture stamp as above. The tree was cut out and shrunk with a heat tool (see page 20). The green mulberry paper was torn to size and glued in place on the card before the gold metal piece, cut with deckle edge scissors, was attached on top with strong glue. Some gold wire coiled into swirls at each end, was slipped under the shrink plastic tree before it was attached with sticky foam pads.

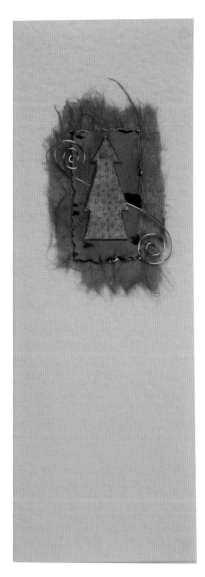

GREEN AND RED LAYERS

You can create a simple and effective design from layers of different coloured card. On this festive design the Swirls and Star image was silver embossed on to first green, then silver mirror card, cut out (leaving only the star on the silver card) and attached with sticky foam pads. This motif was mounted on a pearlescent green card silver embossed with the Dotty Wisp stamp over some torn red card.

Congratulations!

A twenty-first is an important milestone that calls for an extra special card. I still keep all the cards that I received for mine in a box. It is lovely to look back at them and wonder what everyone is doing now. This design contains lots of fun elements, including a wonderful daisy made using a mould, a key charm hung from coiled wire and a stylus-embossed silver panel. It is perhaps better suited to a girl, but you could adapt it for a boy by using a key mould instead of a daisy one.

TECHNIQUE FOCUS

Printing on vellum from a computer is a good way to personalize your card

You will need

- ❖ Ancient Script stamp
- ❖ Small Swirl stamp
- ❖ Orchid Border stamp
- ❖ Ivory hammered card – A4 piece, scored and folded
- ❖ Navy blue card
- ❖ White vellum – one sheet, cut in half
- ❖ Navy blue vellum – 3 x 3.5cm (1¼ x 1½in)
- ❖ Blue scrapbooking paper – 6 x 9.5cm (2½ x 3¾in)
- ❖ Silver print backing paper
- ❖ Daisy Art Mould
- ❖ Delight paperclay
- ❖ Permanent ink pad – black

- ❖ Adirondack dye-based ink pad – denim
- ❖ Embossing ink pad
- ❖ Silver embossing powder
- ❖ Silver metal sheet and stylus embossing tool
- ❖ Silver metal leaf
- ❖ Silver wire – 10cm (4in)
- ❖ Silver brads and puffy hearts
- ❖ Small daisy paper punch
- ❖ Corner rounder punch
- ❖ Silver key charm
- ❖ Point-nosed pliers
- ❖ Needle tool
- ❖ Basic tool kit (see page 8)

See page 126 for product details

21st

Birthday

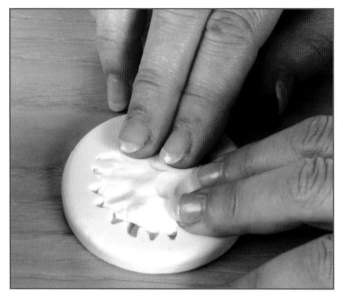

1 Tear off a piece of clay and press it into the mould. Start in the middle of the mould and work towards the edges to eliminate any air bubbles. Leave it in the mould (or carefully remove it), then set aside for about 24 hours to dry.

2 Once it is dry, apply the denim ink pad to the clay daisy until most of the raised areas are covered with ink. Use a heat tool to dry the ink (see page 18).

3 Spray a tiny amount of adhesive over the shape and apply some of the silver leaf. Brush with a soft brush so that the leaf sticks to some parts and allows the blue colour to show through on others.

4 Ink up the Ancient Script stamp with embossing ink and stamp it twice onto the front of the main folded card, once at the top left and again at the lower right. Sprinkle the images with silver embossing powder, tap off the excess and heat.

5 Stamp the Small Swirl image randomly onto the blue vellum using the embossing ink pad, then emboss with silver embossing powder. Cut a piece of silver printed paper slightly larger than the blue vellum.

6 Stamp the Orchid Border image onto the silver metal using the black permanent ink pad. When dry, use the stylus tool to trace over the outline of the image, then turn the piece of metal over.

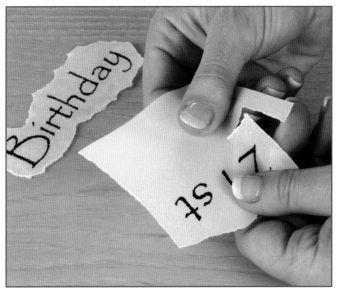

7 Using a computer, print out the words '21st Birthday' on to two separate pieces of white vellum. Roughly tear around the edges of the words '21st' and 'Birthday', leaving enough of a border for fixing them onto the card with brads.

8 Trim the silver metal to about 5 x 1.5cm (2 x ¾in) and use the corner rounder punch on each corner. Twist one end of the silver wire into a spiral with the pliers. Attach the key charm to the spiral by slipping the wire through the loop at the top of the key.

TIP
You can stamp the greeting onto the vellum with a black permanent ink pad or apply peel-offs instead of using a computer if you prefer.

10 Open out the card and arrange the vellum printed with '21st' to the top left of the blue paper. Holding it in place, pierce a hole in one corner with a needle tool in both the vellum and card. Fix a brad through both holes, then do the same in the opposite corner. Repeat with the other two corners. Do the same with the 'Birthday' vellum piece, placing it where it overlaps the blue paper.

9 Using a glue stick, attach the blue printed paper to the centre of the main card. Before it dries, slip the silver printed paper under the bottom left-hand corner and glue down. Apply spray adhesive to the back of the blue vellum and fix it on the right of the blue paper. Attach the stylus embossed metal to the card with spray adhesive, to the lower left of the blue background paper.

To complete the card: Using a sticky foam pad, attach the free end of the wire spiral to the back of the clay daisy, then attach it to the centre of the card. Finally, add three puffy hearts and four punched daisies, as shown.

Wedding Treasures

Mark a special day with a beautiful hand-stamped book filled with treasured photographs and mementoes. The covers were decorated using a set of pretty unmounted wedding stamps with other techniques such as stylus embossing providing the finishing touches. The pages are made from four card blanks joined back to back, and the book is secured with ribbons attached to each cover. This project will be a pleasure to make as well as to receive, and can be adapted to suit another occasion such as an anniversary or christening.

You will need

- ❖ Wedding stamps
  – bells and other motifs
- ❖ Congratulations stamp
- ❖ Triple Tag stamp
- ❖ Four hammered cream card blanks – 12.5cm (5in) square
- ❖ Cream hammered card
- ❖ Mulberry paper
  – pink and cream
- ❖ Mount board – two, 13cm (5¼in) square pieces
- ❖ Fluid Chalk ink pads
  – two shades of pink
- ❖ Black permanent ink pad
- ❖ Embossing ink pad
- ❖ Brush marker pen
  – in a pale colour
- ❖ Silver embossing powder
- ❖ Length of ribbon
- ❖ Assorted fibres
- ❖ Metal sheet – silver, for dry embossing
- ❖ Stylus tool and embossing pad
- ❖ Sponge wedge
- ❖ Photographs and memorabilia
- ❖ Basic tool kit (see page 8)

See page 126 for product details

1 Cut two squares of cream mulberry paper 1cm (½in) larger all round than each mount board piece. Tear strips of the pink and cream mulberry paper to decorate the covers.

2 Apply a thin coat of PVA glue to the front of one cover and add a mulberry paper square. Trim off the corners and dab glue around the edges on the back of the board. Fold the excess paper over and stick down. Repeat with the other cover. Stick the torn strips of mulberry paper from the centre top to centre bottom on each cover, using small amounts of glue and layering a cream strip over a pink one.

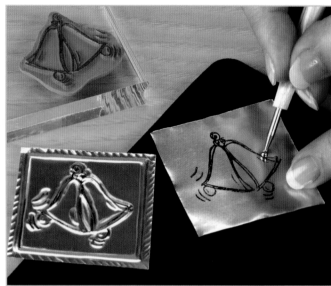

3 Cut a square of metal slightly larger than the bells stamp. Stamp the image on the metal using permanent ink. When dry, place the metal, stamped side up, on a mouse mat or embossing pad and draw firmly over the design with the stylus tool, 'pressing' it into the metal. Draw a frame as well. Turn the metal over and add further small dots and lines to enhance the image with the stylus tool.

4 Ink up a small motif stamp with the pink chalk ink pad and stamp it randomly over the front and back covers. Stamp some of the smaller accent images from the same set using pink ink to fill in the spaces. Carefully align, then stick the metal embellishment to the centre of the front cover with double-sided tape.

5 Decorate the inside of each card blank. Position photographs on a right hand panel, trimming if necessary. Mark four diagonal slits to hold the corners and cut with a craft knife. Cut a piece of mulberry paper to fit the panel. Draw a circle in the centre with a wet paintbrush, and gently tear along the line to make an aperture for the photo. Apply spray mount to the mulberry paper and stick in place.

6 Make a pocket to hold treasures. Cut a 12.5 x 3.5cm (5 x 1½in) strip of card and cover it with mulberry paper, leaving a feathery edge on one long side. Stamp with wedding images in pink ink. Stamp the bride and groom on to more card using embossing ink and silver emboss this image. Cut around it leaving a narrow border all round. Attach the mulberry panel opposite the photo, vertically or across the bottom. Apply double-sided tape to three sides only and add the bride and groom with sticky foam pads.

7 Stamp and cut out tags of varying sizes from the spare cream card using the triple tag stamp with a brush marker. Using a sponge, lightly apply pink ink around the edges of the tags then, using the pink ink pads, stamp some of the small images around the edges. Punch a hole in the top of each tag and push fibres or ribbon through it.

8 Lay the front cover face down on the work surface and attach a length of ribbon across the centre back from one side to the other. Repeat on the back cover. Use double-sided tape to connect all the pieces of the book together, assembling them back to back as in the diagram. You should have four decorated pages facing you and four more decorated pages when you turn the book around.

To complete the keepsake book: Add hand written journalling to the tags, such as quotes, dates, names and places. Insert these into the pockets of the book and add other treasures connected with the occasion, for example pressed flowers from a bouquet or some confetti. Close up the keepsake book by tying the ribbons on the back and front together in a bow on each side.

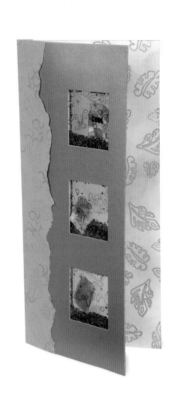

All Shook Up!

Shaker cards make you want to pick them up to see what happens. They are fun and easy to make and ideal for all ages and occasions. This design will bring back happy memories of summer days spent on the beach, relaxing or surfing. Its three apertures are filled with beads and shrink plastic t-shirt motifs that spell out a greeting. You can adapt the size and shape of the apertures to suit the occasion or the stamps you have chosen, but the technique remains the same.

You will need

- ❖ T–shirt stamp
- ❖ Palm Leaves stamp
- ❖ Bubble Line stamp
- ❖ Collage Dotty Wisp stamp
- ❖ Cool stamp
- ❖ Surf stamp
- ❖ Dude stamp
- ❖ Mediterranean blue pearlescent card – A4
- ❖ Lime green card – 6 x 21cm (2½ x 8½in)
- ❖ White shrink plastic
- ❖ Acetate – two, 6 x 18cm (2½ x 7in) strips
- ❖ Fluid Chalk ink pads – lime pastel, ice blue, aquamarine, blue lagoon, azurite, deep green
- ❖ Permanent ink pad – royal blue and black
- ❖ Beadazzles – Electric Slide
- ❖ Square 35mm punch
- ❖ Basic tool kit (see page 8)

See page 126 for product details

TECHNIQUE FOCUS
The idea behind a shaker card is very versatile and can be adapted to suit all ages and occasions.

1 Mark the blue pearlescent card at 10cm intervals on the longest edge. Score with a bone folder down both lines and fold to form a tall card with three panels. With the blue side facing, fold the right-hand panel into the centre. Punch three square holes through both panels.

2 Use the royal blue permanent ink pad to stamp the Bubble Line image all over one acetate strip. Attach the stamped piece of acetate over the back of the three square apertures in the centre panel of the card using double-sided tape. Attach the unstamped piece of acetate over the back of the square apertures in the other panel.

3 Colour enough of the white shrink plastic to fit three of the t-shirt images using any combination of chalk ink pads. Ink up the T-shirt stamp with black permanent ink and stamp three images over the coloured area. Stamp the Palm Leaves images over one of the t-shirts. When dry, cut round it and shrink it with a heat tool (see page 20). Stamp a Surf and Cool image on the other t-shirts and shrink as before.

4 Decorate the card inside panel. Use a torn strip of paper to mask about one third of it next to the fold. Sponge lime pastel chalk ink onto the exposed section and when dry, stamp over it with palm leaves in the same colour ink. Remove the paper mask.

5 Open the card out and lay it face down on a flat surface. Apply sticky foam tape carefully around each aperture in the centre panel of the card. Make sure there are no gaps in the foam tape.

6 Place strips of double-sided tape along the top, bottom and outer edges of the other card panel with apertures. Remove all the backing strips from the sticky foam tape and double-sided tape.

7 Place a mini t-shirt face down in each aperture of the centre section of the card. Add some beads to each aperture, working carefully to avoid getting any on the sticky surfaces. Very carefully bring the outer card panel over to seal both the apertures and the card flap.

8 Score 1cm (½in) in along one long edge of the lime green card and fold along this line. Open it out again and stamp over it randomly with the Palm Leaves image in lime pastel chalk ink pad, and the Collage Dotty Wisp image in aquamarine chalk ink. Tear along the unfolded long edge to create an interesting pattern.

To complete the card: Attach the lime green card to the main card with the torn edge on the front. Add double-sided tape to the top and bottom edges only and down the back of the card.

> ### TIP
> *Fill a shaker card with confetti, rice or small dried flower petals for a wedding.*

Happy Graduation

You can use stamping in scrapbooking to create a unique page that will be treasured for many years. This page celebrates the graduation days of my children, Sam and Mike. I chose a simple blue colour scheme that keeps the photographs as the focus of the page. They included one from when the children were little to give a story to the page. Silver embossed images of antique pens and a Roman plaque complete the page along with the journalling. I kept this to the graduation dates, but you can add further words as well.

You will need

- Roman Plaque stamp
- Antique Dip Pens stamp
- Pen Nibs stamp
- Blue card – two, 12 x 12 sheets
- Dark blue card – A4 sheet
- White card – A4 sheet
- Vellum printed with champagne bottles – one sheet
- Photographs
- Adirondack ink pad – denim
- Embossing ink pad
- Silver embossing powder
- Sizzix die cutting machine
- Sizzix doodle tag number dies
- Invisi dots for vellum
- Glue dots
- Basic tool kit (see page 8)

See page 126 for product details

TECHNIQUE FOCUS
You can either use your chosen photographs as they are or, as I did, scan them into a computer and print them out at the size you need.

1 Use double-sided tape to attach each photograph to white card and trim each one to leave a very narrow border. Then attach them to dark blue card and trim again. The centre photograph was layered first onto one of the 12 x 12 blue card sheets, then onto white and onto dark blue.

2 Tear two pieces of printed vellum to fit across the top of the main page, from the left hand corner, and across the bottom from the right hand corner.

TIP

Don't forget when scrapbooking to always use archival, acid and lignin-free products. These products will not harm your precious photographs. Other types of product could damage them in the long term.

3 Next, ink up the Roman Plaque stamp with the denim ink pad and stamp it twice onto a cut piece from the 12 x 12 blue card.

4 Stamp the Antique Dip Pens image with embossing ink on another cut piece of the 12 x 12 card. Emboss the image with silver embossing powder (see page 18). Silver emboss the Pen Nibs stamp on to more blue card as well.

5 Cut out the two Roman Plaques, each of the individual dip pens, and cut around the Pen Nibs design.

6 Now you have all the pieces for your page, you can play around with the layout. I made the central piece the photograph of both children, and attached it to the page first, using double-sided tape. The two graduation pictures were stuck down, again using tape. Then I attached a Roman Plaque to the top left corner of the centre picture.

7 Attach a torn piece of vellum to the top of the page with Invisi dots. Allow it to overlap the plaque and the photograph in the top corner. Add the vellum across the bottom in the same way, overlapping the photo as before.

8 Add two of the cut out pens at the top of the page and two at the bottom with glue dots. Use double-sided tape to attach the second Roman Plaque to the lower right hand corner of the page. Attach the Pen Nibs image to the vellum in the top left corner of the page.

To complete the card: Just add the journalling. The numbers were cut from dark blue card, using the Sizzix machine and number die and applied in two opposite corners of the page with glue dots.

floral fun

Everyone loves to receive a floral greeting! You can create your own beautiful flowers using easy stamping and moulding techniques to decorate your cards. Details of the stamps and other products used are on page 126.

PENNY'S VASE

Two stamps are used on this subtle design – Penny's Vase and Flower Accents. The vase was stamped on shrink plastic then heated (see page 20), and the flowers were stamped on card and cut out. They were all mounted on green card edged with gold embossing over a piece of mulberry paper. The flower centres and stems are glitter glue.

COILED EFFECT

This vibrant card is fun to make using embossing and wire. The vase was silver embossed on to dark green card using the same Penny's Vase stamp as above, and the flower heads were black embossed on to white card using the Flower Head Border stamp and coloured. Each flower was cut out and attached to silver wire with a sticky foam pad, and stuck to a green panel silver embossed with the scrim side of the double-sided texture stamp. Wire spirals were added between the flowers and the vase stuck on top with a foam pad.

FLOWER BROOCH

The stunning flower head on this brooch was made using Friendly Plastic and a daisy Art Mould. The leaves were made from shrink plastic and were stamped with the Leaf Spray image in gold. Both the flower head and leaves have holes pierced through them (do this to the leaves before heating) for threading gold wire through. A few beads complete the design and there's a pin back behind the flower head.

DAISY VASE

The flower head on this stylish vase design was made in the same way as the brooch above. The vase is made from shrink plastic, and was stamped with the larger image from the Double Vase stamp and the Dotty Wisp image before heating. The flower stem is a piece of wire that was passed through a paper crimper. The main card has a torn sponged edge, and was stamped with Leaf Spray images.

ORCHID PARADE

This stylish card was made using the centre vase from the Double Vase stamp and flower motifs from the Orchid Border stamp. Three vases were stamped onto white shrink plastic and heated with a heat tool. The three flower heads were stamped on purple card and cut out. Each vase was mounted on a pale green card panel stamped with the grid side of a double texture stamp, using sticky foam pads, and trapping a piece of green wire for the stem. The panels were mounted onto patterned paper and attached to a lilac folded card.

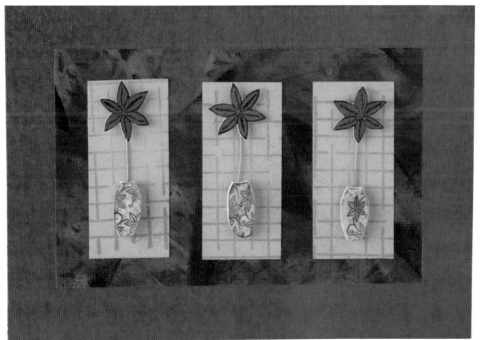

Keep in Touch

Here's a lovely present to make for a student going off to college for the first time. If you include a few stamps you might receive a letter back! The box is made from two sheets of cream card, decorated with writing-related images and glazed with embossing to give a luxuriant look. Inside are six notecards decorated with some of the same images to make a co-ordinated set. Even the envelopes are lined with matching paper. It's all finished off with pretty tags and a wire and bead embellishment and kept together with matching fibres.

You will need

❖ Post Script stamp
❖ Treasured Memories stamp
❖ Antique Dip Pens stamp
❖ Pen Nibs stamp
❖ Triple Scalloped Tag stamp
❖ Double-sided Textured Paper stamp
❖ Plain cream card – three, A4 sheets
❖ Plain white or cream paper
❖ Six cream card blanks – 10.5 x 15cm (4 x 6in)
❖ Six envelopes to match the card blanks
❖ VersaMark ink pad

❖ Fluid Chalk ink pads – amber clay and burnt sienna
❖ VersaFine ink pad – vintage sepia
❖ Gold Encore ultimate metallic ink pad
❖ Clear embossing powder
❖ Copper embossing powder
❖ Decorative fibres
❖ Gold wire
❖ Beads
❖ One small gold brad
❖ Basic tool kit (see page 8)
See page 126 for product details

1 Carefully transfer the template on page 121 for the box top and bottom, onto cream card. The top will fit on one sheet and the bottom on the other sheet. Cut them out and score all the fold lines.

2 Make the box base using strips of double-sided tape. Fold in the corner tabs and secure them in place to bring in the edges of the box. Fold in the last piece and secure inside the base.

3 Apply the amber clay and burnt sienna chalk inks to the box top with a sponge. Pat the sponge on one of the ink pads to pick up some colour, then apply this to the box lid. Repeat with the other colour of ink, using a clean sponge.

4 Use the same chalk colours to ink up the crackle side of the textured paper stamp and apply it randomly onto the card you have just coloured without completely covering it with images. Then use the vintage sepia ink pad to ink up all the other stamps apart from the scalloped tag stamp, and stamp them onto the box top. Ink up one image at a time to prevent the ink drying before you have stamped the image.

5 Apply the VersaMark ink pad directly to the stamped box top, cover it with clear embossing powder and heat with a heat tool (see page 18). Repeat the process to build up a thick layer, adding more VersaMark ink and copper embossing powder in some areas. You may need to add three or four layers. Just before heating the final layer, ink up the Treasured Memories stamp using the gold metallic ink pad and keep it to hand. Heat the final layer of embossing powder and immediately stamp into it with the inked-up stamp. When dry, use strips of double-sided tape to make up the box lid.

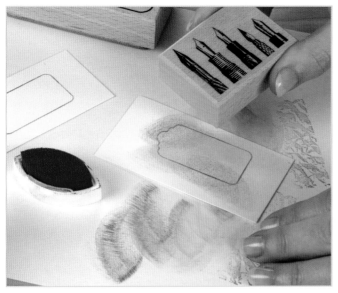

6 Ink up the smallest tag on the Triple Scalloped Tag stamp with burnt sienna chalk ink and stamp two tags onto cream card. Sponge and decorate one using the Pen Nibs stamp and the same ink pad. Cut out the tags. Create a thick layer of copper embossing on the other as in step 5, and stamp the Treasured Memories stamp into the final layer.

7 Fix a piece of card to the inside of both the box lid and box base to strengthen them. Make them the same size as the base and lid and attach with double-sided tape.

8 Use the wire and beads to create an embellishment for the tags. Thread a mixture of beads onto the wire, adding a few spirals in the wire as well by wrapping the wire around a cocktail stick. Then attach the wire embellishment and the two tags to the completed box lid with a brad.

9 Sponge and stamp the paper using the same stamps and ink colours, for lining the envelopes. Lay an open envelope on the stamped paper and cut around the shape. Trim off about 1cm (½in) from the pointed edge on both sides and attach it to the inside of the envelope with double-sided tape or glue.

10 The notecards are made by masking the edges of the card with torn scrap paper to leave a central strip visible. This is stamped with the texture stamp using amber clay chalk ink and embossed with copper embossing powder and the same stamps used on the box lid. You could use a different image on each notecard.

To complete the box: Place the envelopes and cards in the box, then secure the box with the lengths of fibre.

Mosaic Magic

Shrink plastic lends itself well to making mosaic tiles. This is a super technique for creating a stylish frame to display a favourite holiday photograph, or a unique mirror for the bathroom. The tiles are punched from sheets of shrink plastic, coloured and stamped before being heated to shrink them to the right size. They are arranged randomly across the frame and are held in place by paper clay. Any gaps can be filled with shells.

TECHNIQUE FOCUS
This is an ideal project to have on the go. You can make and decorate a batch of tiles whenever it suits you, and store them to use on the frame later.

You will need

- ❖ Orchid Border stamp
- ❖ Palm Trees stamp
- ❖ Palm Leaves stamp
- ❖ Bubble Line stamp
- ❖ Swirl Plaque stamp
- ❖ Double-sided Stars and Swirls Texture stamp
- ❖ Tiny Flower Accents stamp
- ❖ Double-sided Circles and Scrim stamp
- ❖ White shrink plastic – eight or nine sheets
- ❖ Black shrink plastic – one sheet
- ❖ Embossing ink pad
- ❖ Silver embossing powder
- ❖ Fluid Chalk ink pads – dark peony, blue lagoon, aquamarine, French blue, Prussian blue
- ❖ 3.5cm (1½ in) and 5.5cm (2¼ in) square punch
- ❖ Delight paper clay – one pack
- ❖ Old rolling pin
- ❖ Wooden picture or mirror frame
- ❖ Small shells
- ❖ Sanding block
- ❖ Super glue
- ❖ Basic tool kit (see page 8)

See page 126 for product details

1 Take a sheet of white shrink plastic and sand it quite thoroughly with the sanding block, then wipe off any dust with a paper tissue. Punch out about 25 squares using the larger punch. Then punch out about 200 of the smaller squares from sanded white shrink plastic and another 10 from sanded black shrink plastic. You should get 30 of these from each sheet, if you do not leave too much space between each square.

2 Colour the white squares using the chalk ink pads. You can either apply the pads directly to the shrink plastic or use a sponge. Colour some with a light coat of all the shades of blue ink. You can vary the tone, but avoid making it too dark for the stamping to show up. Colour about 20 squares with a very light coat of dark peony ink.

3 Ink up your stamps and stamp them randomly onto the squares. Do about 10 at a time and then heat them, individually, to shrink them (see page 20). Put each batch aside until you have finished them all.

4 Now take the black squares and apply embossing ink all over the surface of each one. Cover with silver embossing powder and heat with a heat tool. Set these pieces aside.

> **TIP**
>
> *If any of the squares do not have enough colour on them, simply pat them with the correct ink pad and leave them to dry.*

5 Take a piece of paper clay and flatten it out on the surface of the wooden frame with your fingers. Cover part of the frame at a time rather than the whole lot in one go. The clay is very soft and will blend together easily.

6 Roll over it with the rolling pin, or an aerosol can, to smooth off the surface a little. Add another piece to the next part of the frame and roll again. Continue doing this until the whole frame is covered, making sure that the clay goes over the edges and covers them completely. Carefully turn the frame over and trim off any pieces of clay, to make it flush with the back edge.

7 Stamp all over the clay with the scrim side of the Double-sided Circles and Scrim stamp. This gives a textural surface similar to rough plaster. Don't forget to stamp around each side, too.

8 Add a little super glue to the back of each square as you work. Group the colours randomly and apply them roughly in straight lines.

9 Fill any gaps that are too small for another square with a shell. Keep applying the squares until the whole of the front of the frame is covered.

To complete the frame: Let your frame dry in a warm dry place for 24 hours. Then go around the edges with Super Glue, sticking any loose pieces of clay back to the wood.

Holiday Memories

Create a scrapbook-style collage panel to hold a precious memory. The idea behind it is similar to making a scrapbook page, because you are capturing a special moment. However, unlike a scrapbook that has to be opened, this can be viewed all the time. All you need to create a piece of wall art you will treasure for years to come, is a simple stretched canvas, a holiday photograph, stamps, embossing powders and moulds, and a few mementoes. You can use the idea to make a fabulous gift for any occasion.

You will need

- ❖ Wavy Lines stamp
- ❖ Swirl Plaque stamp
- ❖ Art Moulds – letters S, E, A, and fossil snail
- ❖ Stretched canvas – 15cm (6in) square
- ❖ Jumbo slide mount or card frame
- ❖ VersaMark ink pad
- ❖ Fluid Chalk ink pads – ice blue, Prussian blue, yellow ochre, amber clay
- ❖ Distress dye-based ink pad – vintage photo
- ❖ PearlEx pigment powders – gold and super russet
- ❖ Thick embossing powder
- ❖ Melt Pot
- ❖ Itty Bitty Beads
- ❖ Decorative fibre
- ❖ Soft Brush
- ❖ Photograph – cut to size
- ❖ Small shells, pebbles or memorabilia
- ❖ Silicone glue
- ❖ Basic tool kit (see page 8)

See page 126 for product details

1 Apply the ice blue, yellow ochre and amber clay chalk ink pads directly to the canvas with a light-handed motion. Apply the blue to the upper two-thirds and a mixture of the others to the lower part. Overlap the blue in the centre with the yellows.

2 Now apply the same colours to the slide mount. Again, use the blue on the upper portion of the mount and the yellows on the lower part, adding the odd touch of yellow over some parts of the blue.

3 Ink up the Wavy Lines stamp with the Prussian blue chalk ink pad and stamp it across the centre of the canvas starting at the right-hand edge. Re-ink the stamp and fill in the gap on the left. Don't worry if it doesn't match up perfectly, as the photograph will cover this later.

4 Apply the dye-based ink to the Swirl Plaque stamp and stamp it across the lower part of the canvas from left to right, below the wavy lines.

5 Apply VersaMark ink to the slide mount, cover it with thick embossing powder and heat to melt (see page 18). Immediately apply more powder and heat again. Do this enough times to build up a thick layer. Just before heating the final layer, ink up the Swirl Plaque stamp with the VersaMark ink pad, heat the final layer of powder and immediately stamp into it with the inked stamp.

6 Heat some thick embossing powder in the Melt Pot. When melted, pour it into the three letter moulds and the fossil snail mould. Let the moulded items cool completely before attempting to remove them.

7 Apply VersaMark ink to the slide mount and to the moulded letters and fossil. Using a soft brush, apply a tiny amount of the gold and super russet pigment powders to colour them.

> **TIP**
>
> *The Melt Pot is a wonderful tool to use with embossing powders. However, the melted powder does become very hot, so it should be used with great care.*

8 Fix the photograph to the canvas in your chosen position with double-sided tape. I positioned mine to the left so that it covers up the join in the wavy line images.

9 Use silicone glue to fix the decorated slide mount over the photograph, securing a length of fibre around the frame at the same time.

To complete the collage panel: Arrange the moulded letters and fossil, the shells and pebbles on the canvas. When you are happy with the way they look, fix them to the canvas with silicone glue. Sprinkle with beads to cover the excess glue.

Shrunk in the Wash

Fun and funky are two words that have maximum appeal to an 18-year-old. Both can be used to describe this birthday card and the special technique used to create it. It features a set of gorgeous miniature clothes hanging on a line made from silver wire. The clothes were created from shrink plastic which was stamped, coloured and cut out before being heated to shrink it.

TECHNIQUE FOCUS

One of the ink pads used on the clothes is a multicoloured one which has a range of shades on the same pad. After heating the colours stand out more strongly.

You will need

- ❖ Happy 18th Birthday stamp
- ❖ Long-sleeved T-shirt stamp
- ❖ Tie-top T-shirt stamp
- ❖ Mini Skirt stamp
- ❖ Frilled Mini Skirt stamp
- ❖ Jeans stamp
- ❖ Ivory hammered card – A5 piece, scored and folded
- ❖ Silver card
- ❖ Cream card
- ❖ Pink mulberry paper
- ❖ White shrink plastic – two sheets
- ❖ Fluid Chalk ink pads – dark peony
- ❖ Brilliance pigment ink pads – twilight and Victorian violet
- ❖ Embossing ink pad
- ❖ Silver embossing powder
- ❖ Silver wire – about 20cm (8in)
- ❖ Silver glitter glue
- ❖ Round-nosed pliers
- ❖ Old wooden board and wooden kebab stick
- ❖ Deckle-edge scissors
- ❖ Sanding block
- ❖ Basic tool kit (see page 8)

See page 126 for product details

Happy
18th
Birthday

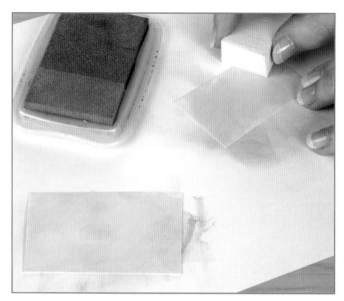

1 Sand the white shrink plastic with the sanding block. You need to be quite thorough, working in both directions and also in a circular motion. Wipe the sheet with a tissue to clean off any dust. Then, using a sponge, apply some lavender from the twilight pigment ink pad to one end of the sanded shrink plastic. Stamp a tie-top t-shirt, a mini skirt and some jeans on the coloured shrink plastic, using the Victorian violet ink pad.

TIP

When sanding shrink plastic, try to avoid leaving any deep or obvious lines as ink tends to bleed into these.

2 Sponge some pink ink from the twilight ink pad on the other piece of shrink plastic. Then stamp a long-sleeved t-shirt and a frilled mini skirt on it, using the dark peony chalk ink pad.

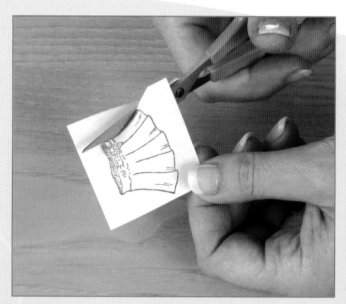

3 Cut around each item of clothing using a pair of small scissors. Leave a small border around the edge rather than trying to cut exactly up to the line. Take great care when cutting as the ink will still be wet.

4 Heat each piece separately on the wooden board, making sure they don't stick together as they shrink. Hold the plastic down with a kebab stick to stop it being blown away. When it flattens itself out, the shrinking process is complete (see page 20).

Shrunk in the Wash

5   Apply small sticky foam pads to the back of each piece of clothing and some silver glitter glue to the front.

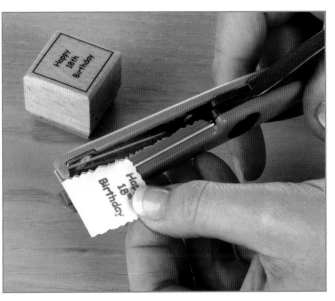

7   Stamp and silver emboss the words 'Happy 18th Birthday' on a small piece of cream card. Trim with deckle-edge scissors. Mount on to a piece of silver card and trim the edges, leaving a small border.

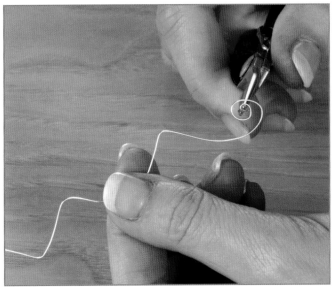

6   Curl up each end of the silver wire into a spiral using the pliers. Bend it at intervals along the length to make it wavy as well.

8   Tear a strip of pink mulberry paper to fit across the centre of the card and stick down as shown, with spray mount. Trim off the excess paper at either end of the card. Place the wavy line of wire on top of the mulberry paper.

9   Use sticky foam pads to stick the shrunk jeans in the centre of the line, trapping the wire between the foam pad and the card. Add the other shrunk clothes so that the colour alternates from lavender to pink across the washing line.

To complete the card: Stick the 'Happy 18th' panel in the bottom right-hand corner using double-sided tape.

animal magic

Animals are a popular theme in card making. Here is a selection of different ways of showing animals on your designs. Turn to page 127 for details of the products used.

SOUND OF THE SEA

The edges on this unusual nautical card have been cut into a fancy pattern. The background was stamped randomly with the Sea Life Elements stamp and the scrim side of the Double-sided Circles and Scrim stamp using two shades of blue dye-based ink. It is decorated with shrink plastic embellishments stamped with the Sea Life and Bubble Line images, and beads and charms, threaded on turquoise wire and fixed to the card with brads.

CLOUD OF BUTTERFLIES

This beautiful butterfly was made from Friendly Plastic and an Art Mould with spirals of black wire for the antennae. It was attached with sticky foam pads onto silver pearlescent card randomly embossed with a small butterfly stamp, layered onto first white then dark pink card.

FRIENDLY LION

This quick card was made with the QuicKutz die cutting system and a set of Zoo dies. The lion was cut from light brown and cream paper, and stuck over two strips torn from tan and pearlescent ivory paper. The tan paper was stamped with the Double-sided Crackle and Textured Paper stamp in dark brown ink and edged with a brown marker pen. The tail was created by trapping a few fibres.

FESTIVE ELEPHANT

Like the butterfly opposite, the elephant on this card was made using an Art Mould and Delight clay. It was painted black when dry and further highlights added with blue PearlEx powder and glitter glue. The burgundy background card was covered with a vertical strip of paler handmade paper and then stamped with the Quilt Mosaic stamp in black permanent ink, and coloured with a PearlEx Palette. You will need a strong glue to attach the elephant to the card.

DOLLY THE SHEEP

The cute motif in the top left of this design was made using the Dolly the Sheep stamp with a dark pink pigment ink pad. The image was embossed with clear embossing powder, cut out and sponged lightly with ink from a pink ink pad before being stuck to pink pearlescent card and cut into a rectangle. The flower in the bottom right corner is a silver peel-off applied to another rectangle of pink card. The squares were cut from purple pearlescent card using a paper punch and attached with double-sided tape.

FROM THE GARDEN

In the centre of this unusual card is a panel of silver metal stamped with the Garden Elements stamp using embossing ink and embossed with pearlescent white embossing powder. The words underneath are from the same stamp. Each flower panel was attached with four brads to lilac card. This was stuck to the card with foam pads. The words were taped directly to the card.

Precious Little Pages

This tiny, pocket-sized, leather bound book is perfect for filling with favourite pictures as a special gift for a husband, father, grandfather – or anyone you want to create one for. It's easy to make using slide mounts and a leather texture stamp. You can keep the design simple or dress it up to suit an occasion. It will make a wonderful book of treasured memories.

TECHNIQUE FOCUS

You can either buy your slide mounts from a craft shop or make your own using the templates on page 120.

You will need

- ❖ Double-sided Abstract/ Leather Texture stamp
- ❖ Pocket Watch stamp
- ❖ Treasured Memories stamp
- ❖ Secret Keys stamp
- ❖ Five, fold-over card slide mounts
- ❖ Light coloured natural unpolished leather to fit the template on page 120
- ❖ Fluid Chalk ink pad – amber clay
- ❖ Distress dye-based ink pads – old paper, antique linen, vintage photo

- ❖ Clear embossing powder
- ❖ Copper embossing powder
- ❖ Knitting ribbon or other fibre with a slight stretch
- ❖ ⅛in hole punch
- ❖ Wax leather polish – natural
- ❖ Photos – to fit the slide mounts
- ❖ Optional embellishments – wire, brads, beads
- ❖ Basic tool kit (see page 8)

See page 127 for product details

1 Start by preparing the slide mounts. Using a sponge, apply ink from the chalk ink pad to the front of each mount. Ink up the Leather Texture stamp with the old paper dye-based ink and stamp it over the chalk colour on the slide mount. Repeat with the antique linen ink pad. You can stop here, but to achieve the full darker effect, ink the stamp again with the vintage photo dye-based ink and apply over the first two shades. Repeat this process on all the slide mounts.

2 Trace the template for the book cover from page 120 onto the back of your leather, then cut it out and punch the two holes in it. On the smooth side, stamp the Leather Texture image using the antique linen dye-based ink.

> **TIP**
> *You can either allow the ink layers to dry naturally or apply some clear and/or metallic embossing powder to the mounts at any stage before they are completely dry. This will give a lovely glazed finish.*

3 Stamp the following images onto the cover – Treasured Memories word stamp, Secret Keys and Pocket Watch – using the vintage photo dye-based ink. Arrange them as desired, without overlapping. Once the ink is completely dry, polish the leather with the natural wax polish. This will seal the images and help to protect the leather.

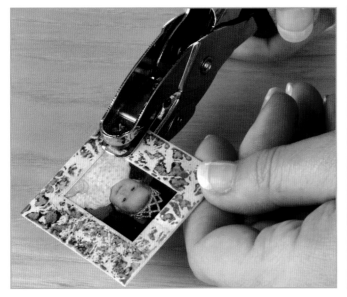

4 To assemble the book, cut one of the slide mounts in half and mount a photo in each half. Fix one to the inside of the front cover and one to the inside of the back cover with double-sided tape. Leave a 1.5cm (¾in) space between them for the other mounts. Mount a photo in each side of the other four slide mounts, fold and stick them closed. Punch two, ⅛in holes in each mount, one 1.25cm (½in) down from the top and one 1.25cm (½in) up from the bottom, both 0.5cm (¼in) in from the inside edge.

5 Thread a piece of your chosen fibre through the top hole in the cover, through the top hole in each slide mount and out again through the top hole in the cover. Link the pieces together through the lower hole in the same way. Turn the book over and knot the fibres securely at the centre of the spine. Pull the threads fairly tight but allow for the pages to be turned inside.

TIP
You can further embellish your finished book with brads, wire, beads, buttons, tiny tags and more stamped words. It's the perfect excuse for turning out your craft cupboard to see what you can find.

6 To form the book closure, take two of the lengths of fibre at the spine, pass them around opposite sides of the book, and knot them together at the opening edge. This loop can be slipped off to open the book and put back on to secure it.

To complete the book: Repeat step 6, using the other two lengths of fibre. Then simply knot some beads onto the ends of the fibres.

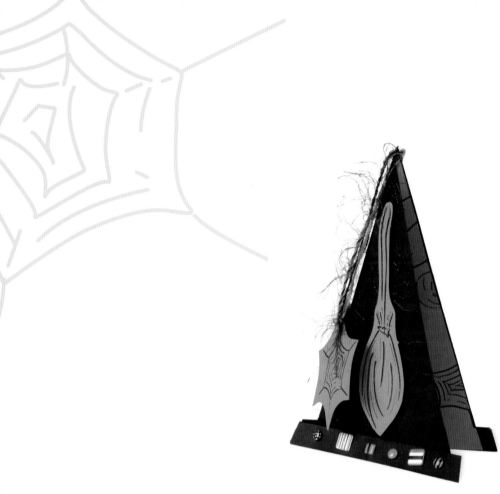

Halloween Hat

Black and orange are two colours we associate with Halloween, and they look stunning together on this versatile design. You can use it to make the invitations for a Halloween party or to decorate the party room or food table. If you scale it up in size, it could even be turned into a set of Halloween party hats. The hat is embossed with ghostly motifs, and decorated with ghostly stamped motifs cut from contrasting paper, and tiny brads on a Halloween theme.

You will need

- ❖ Broomstick stamp
- ❖ Cobweb stamp
- ❖ Witch's Hat stamp
- ❖ Pumpkin stamp
- ❖ Black card – A4 sheet
- ❖ Orange card
- ❖ Distress ink pad
    – black soot
- ❖ Clear embossing powder
- ❖ Black and orange fibres

- ❖ Textured Trio brads
    – Halloween
- ❖ Needle tool
- ❖ Stylus tool
- ❖ Ruler
- ❖ Hole punch
- ❖ Sticky foam pads
- ❖ Basic tool kit (see page 8)

See page 127 for product details

TECHNIQUE FOCUS
You can create a striking effect by cutting your cards into an unusual shape. I couldn't resist making my Halloween design into a witch's hat.

1 Draw round the witch's hat template on page 123 on to black card and cut it out. You should be able to get two cards from one A4 sheet.

2 Using the stylus tool and a ruler, score down the centre line and the two lines across the bottom.

4 Now fold along the lower scored line on each side, this time folding the card down instead of up.

3 Cut up the central line from the bottom of the card for about 2.5cm (1in). Fold up the upper scored line on first the front, then the back of the card.

TIP

Snipping at the base will make it easier to fold up the brim of the hat one side at a time. If you don't do this, you could tear the card.

5 Draw round the hat template on orange card and cut out the triangle shape up to the first fold line. Check it fits neatly inside the black card, trimming more if necessary.

6 Stamp the cobweb, witch's hat and pumpkin images
   randomly over the front of the black card with
embossing ink, allowing some to go over the edges. Sprinkle
the images with clear powder and heat (see page 18). Stamp
the same images on to the orange triangle with the black
soot ink pad and heat emboss with clear powder.

7 Stamp the broomstick and cobweb images on a
   separate piece of orange card using black ink. Heat
emboss with clear powder, then cut out the images. Mount
the broomstick on the front of the card with foam pads.

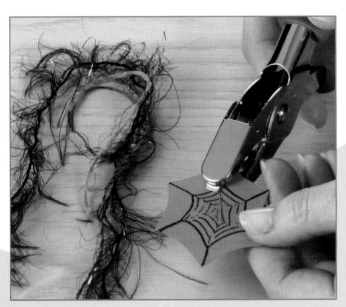

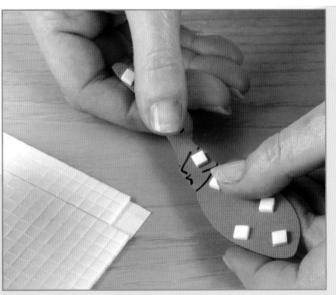

9 Fix the orange triangle insert to the right-hand panel
   inside the card, using double-sided tape.

8 Punch a hole in the cobweb, thread through some
   orange and black fibres and knot the end on the back.
Stick the other end of the fibres to the inside of the card at
the point of the hat.

To complete the hat: Use a
needle tool to pierce a row of
holes along the outside flap
of the hat brim and attach
a Halloween brad in each
one. Then stick the flap
down with strong glue, and
attach the brim to the card.

Halloween Hat

103

On the Move

Everyone loves to receive a card from their family and friends when they're moving house. Here's a really special design to make for someone who's on the move, or to let your friends know your own new address. An acetate sheet printed with the words 'New Home' and held in place by four brads, separates the stamped house from the pretty stamped background beneath. The 3D effect is completed by sticking a second layer of windows on the house.

You will need

❖ Town House stamp
❖ Decorative Flower stamp
❖ Swirl Leaf stamp
❖ Tiny Flower Accents stamp
❖ Leaf Spray stamp
❖ Ivory hammered card
  – 12.5cm (5in) square
  when folded
❖ Cream card
❖ Orange mulberry paper
❖ Ink jet printer acetate

❖ Marvy Le Plume pens – red,
  light green, dark brown,
  pine green, yellow, blue
❖ Embossing ink pad
❖ Gold embossing powder
❖ Clear embossing powder
❖ Permanent ink pad – brown
❖ Four brass eyelets
❖ Punch and setter
❖ Basic tool kit (see page 8)
See page 127 for product details

TECHNIQUE FOCUS
You can stamp the words on the acetate instead of printing them with a computer if you prefer. This can be done using a permanent ink pad for lasting effects.

1 Using any graphics programme on a computer, type the words 'New Home' enough times to form a random group in the centre of the document. Print a test sheet to check the words are the right size for the card and correctly positioned, then print it out again in dark brown on a sheet of acetate.

2 Stamp and gold emboss the Decorative Flower, Leaf Spray, Swirl Leaf and Tiny Flower Accents around the edges of the front of the card. Take the red and two green pens and scribble some of each colour on to a palette. With a damp paintbrush, pick up the colour and paint all the leaves and flowers.

3 Tear a rough square of orange mulberry paper and stick it to the centre of the painted card with spray mount.

4 Trim your printed acetate so that it is the same size as your square card. Place it over the card, and punch a hole in each corner for the eyelets using the correct size for your eyelet. Insert an eyelet in each hole, turn the card over and hammer it flat with the fixing tool.

TIP

To tear mulberry paper, first paint a strip of water and then gently pull the paper apart along the wet line. This will give a pretty feathery finish when dry.

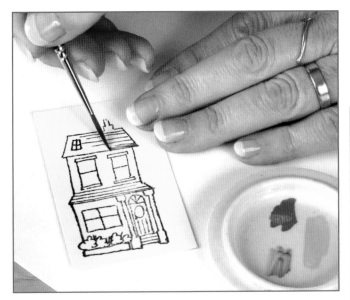

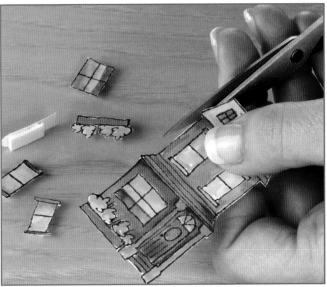

5 Stamp the Town House stamp twice on to cream card with the brown permanent ink pad. Heat emboss with clear powder (see page 18). Paint one of the images using the red pen as before, adding some dark brown to the edges and leaving the windows, window box, and front door blank. Colour only these items on the second image using the red, yellow and blue pens.

6 Cut out the whole of the red house, and just the coloured in windows, front door and window box on the second house.

7 Attach the second set of windows, front door and window box directly on top of the ones on the coloured-in house, using sticky foam pads.

To complete the card: Add more sticky foam pads to the back of the house and stick this to the acetate in the centre of the words.

TIP

Use a glue stick or spray mount when bonding mulberry paper to another surface. If you use a glue that is too wet, the mulberry paper will become soaked and lose its fine, soft texture.

celebrations

Sensationally simple...

A celebration such as a christening or a twenty-first calls for a very special card. I hope this selection of designs will inspire you to create your own unique card. Details of the products used are on page 127.

WELCOME TAG

Here's a stylish way to present a welcome gift. This lovely tag was stamped randomly with the Leaf Spray stamp using green ink, and embellished with a shrink plastic tag stamped with the New Home image. This was also sponged with green ink, stamped with the scrim side of the Double-sided Circles and Scrim Stamp in brown ink, and finished with a flower button. The word 'welcome' can either be hand written or stamped, and the tag is threaded with a piece of raffia.

FULSOME 40TH

A rich-coloured patterned paper and gold embossing with the Magic Carpet stamp set the tone for this stunning fortieth birthday design. In the centre is a decoration made from Friendly Plastic and a square Art Mould. The greeting was printed onto vellum and has a torn edge. Below it is a mini gold metal plaque stamped with the Ancient Script image using a permanent ink pad, and embossed with a stylus. Another vellum panel is embossed with the Bubble Line image. Gold stars, brads and coiled wire add the finishing touches that make the design look so special.

HAPPY 18TH

This 18th birthday tag features a key made from Friendly Plastic and an Art Mould, and flowers stamped on gold metal with the Mini Flowers image and embossed with a stylus tool. The stamped greeting is attached with brads over gingham paper.

Celebrations

108

PRECIOUS BABY

This elegant blue and silver card has two silver embossed panels – one with the Baby Rattle image stamped on dark blue card and edged with silver, and the other with the Precious Baby word stamp embossed on a torn strip of vellum. The greeting was embossed with a stylus tool on a silver metal panel. The vellum is layered over a sponged blue background strip.

ON YOUR CHRISTENING

The same Precious Baby stamp was silver embossed on the background of this christening card, along with the Baby Clothes Line image. Layered on top of mulberry paper is a panel with a baby photo, a silver embossed and coloured, cut out Baby Pram, and a vellum greeting.

SPECIAL THANK YOU

The background on this thank you card was stamped with the Bubble Line, Orchid Border and Decorative Flower images. These were also stamped on to shrink plastic, cut into frame shapes and heated to make miniature frames, and filled with more images stamped on card. A handful of buttons finishes off the design.

KEY TO THE DOOR

The key on this twenty-first card is made using Friendly Plastic and an Art Mould. The greeting is stylus embossed on to a small square of gold metal and stuck to a larger square of floral patterned paper. The background is created from gold embossed swirls and turquoise and orange mulberry paper. The number 21 was printed onto vellum and attached with two brads. Gold stars, punched dragonflies and a spiral of gold wire with a charm add the finishing touches.

Beautiful Bag

What a delightful way to receive a gift – presented in a gorgeous handmade bag decorated with stamping and embellishments. It will almost make a gift on its own, and is certainly a work of art. It features a leaf swirl made from layers of gold embossing and many other special pieces. You can adapt the template to make your bag any size you want.

TECHNIQUE FOCUS
A project like this lovely bag lends itself to using any beads, charms, embellishements or found objects like shells, old jewellery and buttons, you may already have.

You will need

- ❖ Decorative Flower stamp
- ❖ Swirl Leaf stamp
- ❖ Tiny Flower Accents stamp
- ❖ Small Swirl stamp
- ❖ Tiny Thank You stamp
- ❖ Handmade mulberry paper – lime, dark green
- ❖ Green vellum – A4 sheet
- ❖ Brilliance pigment ink pad – pearlescent ivy
- ❖ Distress dye-based ink pad – peeled paint
- ❖ Adirondack dye-based ink pad – espresso
- ❖ Gold PearlEx pigment ink pad
- ❖ Embossing ink
- ❖ Gold and dark green embossing powder
- ❖ Small green skeleton leaves
- ❖ Large daisy punch
- ❖ Gold Krylon pen
- ❖ Lumiere paint – emerald
- ❖ Green eyelash fibre – two, 45cm (18in) lengths
- ❖ Metal rim tags – one large, one small
- ❖ ⅛in hole punch
- ❖ Non-stick craft sheet
- ❖ Super glue gel
- ❖ Basic tool kit (see page 8)

See page 127 for product details

1 Enlarge the gift bag template on page 119 to fit on an A4 sheet, and cut it out. Position the template on the sheet of green vellum and draw round it, marking the fold lines with a pencil, then cut it out. Score all the lines with a bone folder and ruler. Fold along each of them to crease the paper, then open out the sheet again ready to decorate it.

2 Stamp the Decorative Flower four times over the vellum using embossing ink. Sprinkle with gold embossing powder and heat (see page 18). Tear off some strips of lime and dark green mulberry paper and stick them randomly onto the bag using spray mount. Go over the paper with a wet paintbrush before tearing it.

3 Fold the top strip over so that it will be on the inside of the bag and glue it in place.

4 Pour a level teaspoon of gold embossing powder on the non-stick craft sheet. Pour about half this amount of green embossing powder on top. Ink up the Swirl Leaf stamp with embossing ink and leave it on the ink pad until required.

5 Turn on the heat tool, pointing it away from the powder. Hold it 45cm (18in) above the powder, where it doesn't blow it around. Hold it here for a few seconds then lower it a little. Hold this position for a few more seconds then lower again. Keep doing this until you are at normal height. By now the powder should have melted just enough to stick. As soon as it has melted fully, place the Leaf Swirl stamp on top and press down gently. Leave to cool for five minutes. Carefully lift off the stamp from the melted powder and you should have a lovely stamped piece. Handle carefully as it will be fragile. Make another piece the same way.

6 Attach a couple of skeleton leaves to the bag using spray mount. Ink up the Tiny Flower Accents stamp with the pearlescent ivy ink and stamp randomly over the bag. With the large daisy punch, punch out two daisies from the plain copier paper and paint them with the emerald green paint. Allow to dry and then sponge on a little of the gold ink. Once dry, stick the flowers to the bag using double-sided tape or glue.

7 With embossing ink, stamp the Small Swirl all over the bag, overlapping the mulberry paper in places. Emboss the images with gold powder. Then apply a few spots of super glue to the back of your fragile embossing pieces and stick one on each side of the bag.

8 Attach a piece of double-sided tape down one side of the bag. Remove the tape backing and stick it to the opposite side to form the bag shape. Fold in the bottom four pieces to see where you need to apply glue, then stick them in place using a glue stick.

9 Punch two holes on each side of the bag at the top. Thread a length of fibre through both holes on one side of the bag. Pull up enough in the centre to form a handle and tie a knot at each hole to secure, leaving two ends hanging outside the bag. Repeat on the other side.

10 Take the two metal rim tags and apply some of the peeled paint ink with a sponge onto both sides of each one. Stamp and gold emboss the Tiny Thank You image on one side of the larger tag. Stamp it again on the other side with the espresso ink. Cover the words with a clear domed sticker. Add a flower sticker to one side of the smaller tag.

To complete the bag: Colour some of the edges with the gold pen. Then thread some beads and charms on to the hanging fibres and tie them in place along the length. Tie on a tag on each side of the bag and embellish with any other found objects, such as shells or buttons.

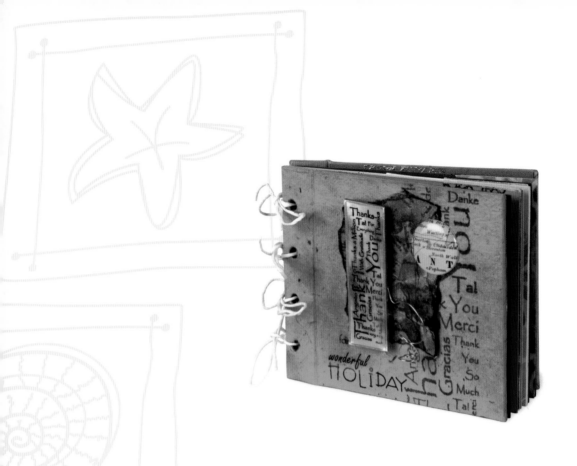

Mini Scrapbook

A pretty mini scrapbook makes an unusual way to thank someone special and is ideal for sharing the memories of a happy time spent with family or friends. Once you have made one book, you'll want to do more because decorating the pages is such fun! You will find a series of ready cut ones in a mini scrapbook kit. If you scan your photographs into a computer you can print them out at any size you like, or you can do this on a photocopier.

You will need

❖ Thank You Text stamp
❖ Tiny Flower Accents stamp
❖ New Home stamp
❖ Sea Life Elements stamp
❖ Collage Pebbles stamp
❖ Decorative Flower stamp
❖ Collage swirls stamp
❖ Mini scrapbook kit
❖ Assorted papers
❖ Map design paper
❖ Orange mulberry paper
❖ White shrink plastic
❖ Domed stickers
❖ Alphabet stickers or stamps
❖ Ink jet printer acetate
❖ Embossing ink pad
❖ Gold embossing powder
❖ Adirondack dye-based ink pads – currant and steam
❖ Permanent ink pad – timber brown
❖ Fluid Chalk ink pads – burnt sienna and amber
❖ Raffia or fibres
❖ Gold wire
❖ Gold brads
❖ Gold Krylon pen
❖ Point nose pliers
❖ Xyron machine and adhesive cartridge
❖ Basic tool kit (see page 8)

See page 127 for product details

1 Cut two pieces of orange mulberry paper slightly larger than the covers in the mini scrapbook kit. Spray one with adhesive and position the first cover, face down, in the centre. Cut diagonally across each corner, stopping short of the corner of the card cover. Fold over one side of the paper and stick it down. Repeat with the opposite side and then the other two sides. Repeat with the other book cover. Take two of the mini scrapbook pages and stick one to the inside of each cover to hide the turned down edges.

2 Cover the two binding strips from the kit with mulberry paper in the same way as the covers. Re-punch the holes with an awl or other pointed tool.

5 Tear off a piece of map paper and age it by applying the chalk ink pads directly to the surface. Ink up the Thank You Text stamp with timber brown ink and stamp it on one side of the map paper.

3 On a computer type some words relevant to your subject, for example place names for a holiday book. Print them on to acetate using the mirror image option. You can also print out any clip art, such as ice creams or suns.

4 Re-size a number of photographs on the computer to fit the pages of the book and print these out on paper. This can also be done on a photocopier. Trim the photographs and run them through a Xyron machine to apply an even layer of adhesive to the back.

6 Dab burnt sienna ink, straight from the pad, onto a piece of shrink plastic, then stamp the Thank You image on top with timber brown ink. Place it on a wooden board and gently hold in place with a kebab stick. Apply the heat tool so that it shrinks (see page 20) and, when cool, run the gold pen around the edges.

7 Cut a piece of gold wire about 5cm long and twist one end into a spiral. Cut out some of the acetate words and stick them and the stamped piece of map, to the front cover of the book with spray adhesive. Attach the shrunk 'thank you' tile using a sticky foam pad, trapping the spiral of wire behind it. Add the domed sticker.

8 Cut pieces of backing paper to stick to the pages inside the book. Avoid applying one to every page or covering the whole of a page as the photographs should be the main focal points.

9 Go through the pages, stamping at random using all the stamps and the dye-based and permanent ink pads. You can also stamp some with embossing ink and emboss them with gold embossing powder (see page 18).

10 Stick a photograph, or part of one, to each page, covering parts of some pictures with more stamps.

To complete the scrapbook: Put all the pages together and line up all the holes. Cut some lengths of raffia and thread them through the holes to tie the book together to complete your mini scrapbook.

Templates

Here are the templates you will need for some of the projects in the book. You can either trace them on to card or scale them up on a photocopier.

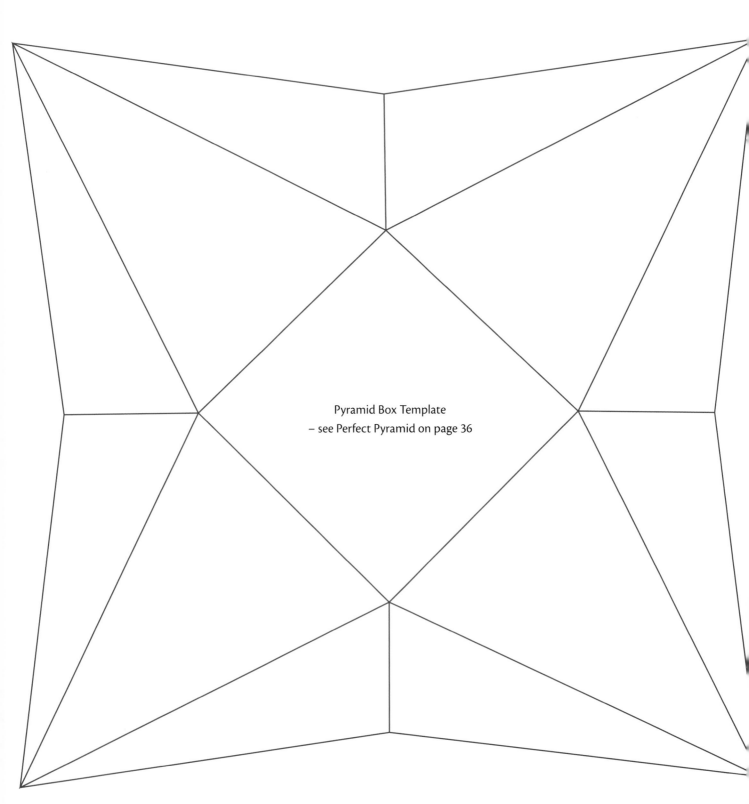

Pyramid Box Template
– see Perfect Pyramid on page 36

Gift Bag Template – see Beautiful Bag on page 110

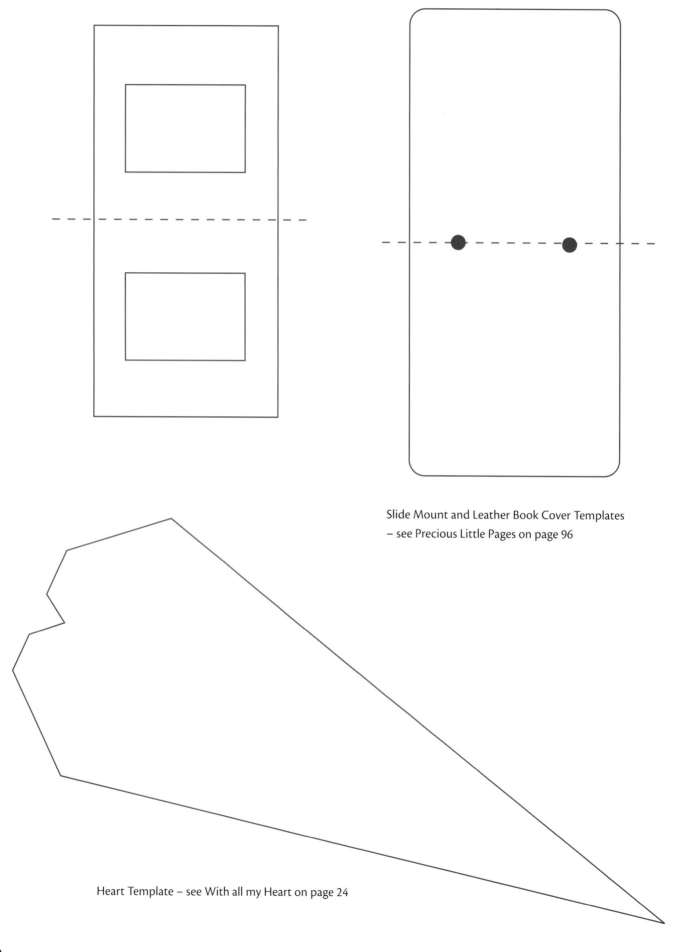

Slide Mount and Leather Book Cover Templates
– see Precious Little Pages on page 96

Heart Template – see With all my Heart on page 24

Cutting and Folding Template for the Notecard Box
– see Keep in Touch on page 78

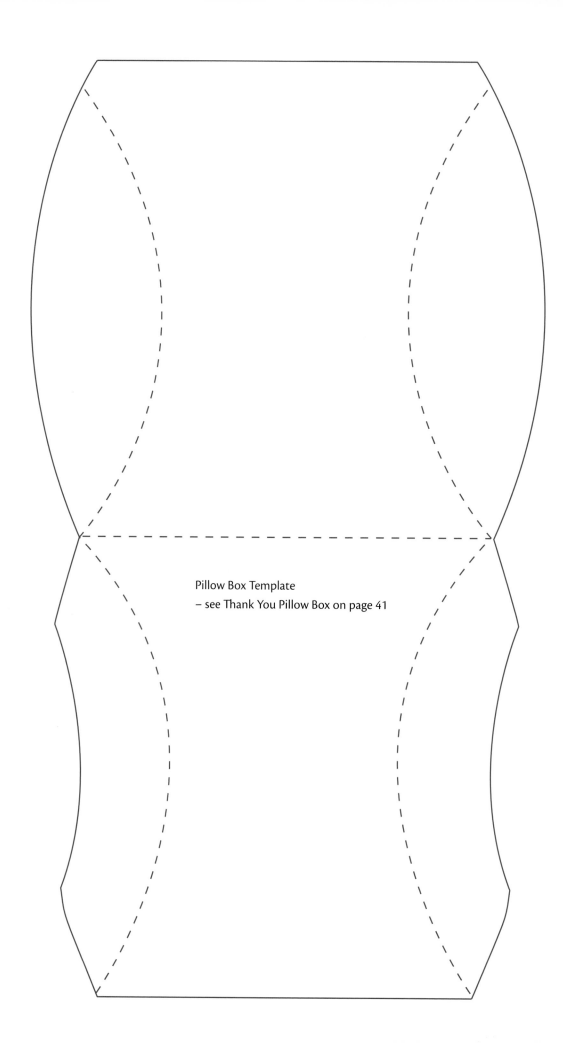

Pillow Box Template
– see Thank You Pillow Box on page 41

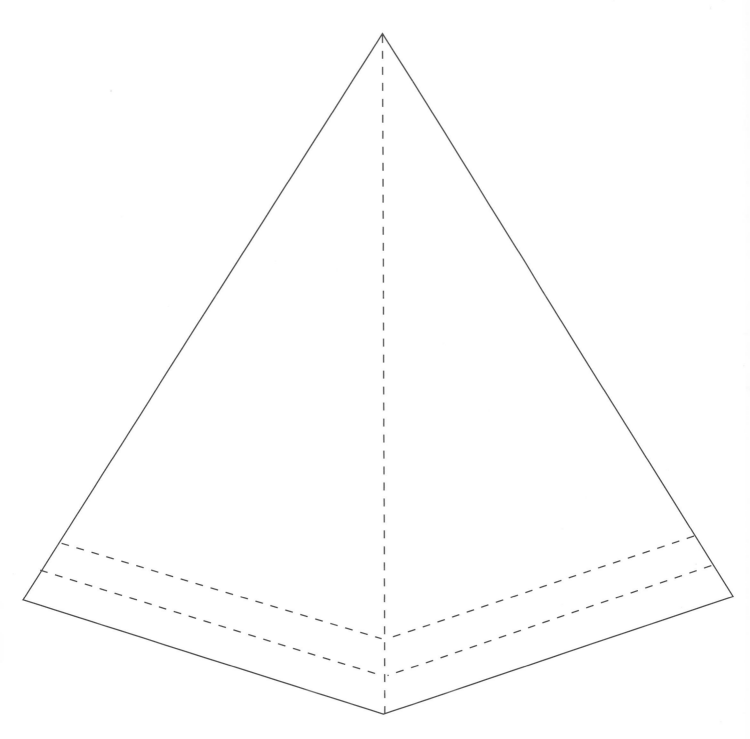

Cutting and Folding Template
– see Halloween Hat on page 100

Products and Suppliers

Throughout the book I have used stamps from Artifacts, which is a range of stamps that my husband and I produce. To this end I know that they will all still be available and will not go out of production. It should also be noted that we do make a much larger range of stamps and we can make the stamps up in other languages if need be. We ship world-wide.

Artifacts stamps are only available from:

The Stamp Bug Ltd
3 and 4 Hatherop
Near Cirencester
Gloucestershire
GL7 3NA   United Kingdom
Telephone and Fax:
01285 750308
email:
jane@thestampbug.co.uk
On-line shop:
www.thestampbug.co.uk

The Art Moulds used in some projects are available from The Stamp Bug Ltd, address above.
They are manufactured by Krafty Lady, Australia.
www.kraftylady.co.au
The Powder Keg embossing powders are available in the UK from The Stamp Bug Ltd.

We have used other products from the following manufacturers, all of which are available from The Stamp Bug Ltd and other stamp retailers.

USA

Clearsnap Inc
PO Box 98
Anacortes WA 98221
Tel: 360-293-6634
www.clearsnap.com
Fluid Chalk ink pads

EK Success
261 River Road
Clifton   NJ 07014
Tel: 800-524-1349
www.eksuccess.com
Paper punches

K&Company
8500 NW River Drive
Pillar 136
Parkville   MO 64152
Tel: 816-389-4150
www.kandcompany.com
Background papers; stickers

Lucky Squirrel
PO Box 606
Belen   NM 87002
Tel: 800-462-4912
www.luckysquirrel.com
Shrink plastic

The Powder Keg
www.apapergarden.com
Embossing powder

Ranger Industries Inc
15 Park Road
Tinton Falls   NJ 07724
Tel: 732-389-3535
www.rangerink.com
Alcohol Inks; Alcohol Ink
Applicator Tool; Distress ink
pads; Adirondack ink pads

Stampendous Inc
1240 North Road Gum
Anaheim   CA 92806
Tel: 714-688-0288
Embossing powders

Tsukineko Inc
17640 NE 54th Street
Redmond   WA 98052
Tel: 425-883-7733
www.tsukineko.com
VersaMark ink pads; VersaFine
ink pads; Brilliance ink pads;
Encore ink pads; Melting Pot

Uchida of America Corp
3535 Del Amo Boulevard
Torrance   CA 90503
Tel: 310-793-2200
www.uchida.com
Marvey brush pens; Le Plume
pens; StazOn permanent
ink pads

USArtQuest Inc
7800 Ann Arbor Road
Grass Lake   MI 49240
Tel: 517-522-6225
www.usartquest.com

The Stamper's, Scrapbooker's and Papercrafter's Guild.

In July 2006 Jane started The Stamper's, Scrapbooker's and Papercrafter's Guild. Members can enjoy regular newsletters, offers, discounts and special Guild Days, plus more! Please visit the web site at www.thesspguild.com for further information about this world-wide Guild of crafters.

Product Details
Listed here are the stamps and other products used for each project.

With all my Heart – page 24
Double-sided Stars & Swirls stamp – A/F X002

Precious Baby – page 28
Baby Rattle stamp – A/F B059
Collage Dotty Wisp stamp – A/F B064
Precious Baby stamp – A/F G022

Spirit of Adventure – page 32
Spirit of Adventure stamp – A/F G030
Describe Him stamp – A/F G023

Perfect Pyramid – page 36
Orchid Border stamp – A/F D015
Time in Motion stamp – A/F E033
Ancient Script stamp – A/F G018
Small oval tag Art Mould – AM188

Bags and Boxes – page 40
Pen Nibs stamp – A/F D028
Time in Motion stamp – A/F E033
Postscript stamp – A/F G028
Ancient Script stamp – A/F G018
T-shirt stamp – A/F E022
Shorts stamp – A/F E023
Surfing stamp – A/F B023
Cool stamp – A/F B056
Double-sided Stars & Swirls stamp – A/F X002
Small Swirls stamp – A/F A001
Thank You stamp – A/F C005
Geometric stamp – A/F X004
Butterfly stamps – A/F A043, B022

Star Qualities – page 42
Describe Him stamp – A/F G023

Origami Blue – page 46
Double-sided Stars & Swirls stamp – A/F X002

Star Delight – page 50
Double-sided Geometric stamp – A/F X004
Ancient Script stamp – A/F G018
Collage Splatter stamp – A/F B063
Sea Life Elements stamp – A/F G010
Collage Swirls stamp – A/F B060
Swirls stamp – A/F B021

Pretty Wrapping – page 54
Starry Christmas Tree stamp – A/F E011
Swirls and Star stamp – A/F E013
Small Star stamp – A/F A002
Triple Tag stamp – A/F H004

Christmas Creations – page 58
Snowflake stamp – A/F D012
Christmas Crown stamp – A/F E014
Small Star stamp – A/F A002
Double-sided Stars & Swirls stamp – A/F X002
Dotty Wisp stamp – A/F B064
Swirls and Star stamp – A/F E013

Congratulations! – page 60
Ancient Script stamp – A/F G018
Small Swirl stamp – A/F A001
Orchid Border stamp – A/F D015
Daisy Art Mould – AM157
StazOn permanent ink pad – black

Wedding Treasures – page 64
Unmounted wedding stamp set – A/F U001
Congratulations stamp – A/F C004
Triple Tag Stamp – A/F H004

All Shook Up! – page 68
T-shirt stamp – A/F E023
Palm Leaves stamp – A/F D017
Bubble Line stamp – A/F C031
Collage Dotty Wisp stamp – A/F B064
Cool stamp – A/F B056
Surf stamp – A/F B023
StazOn permanent ink pad – royal blue

Happy Graduation – page 72
Roman Plaque stamp – A/F F005
Antique Dip Pens stamp – A/F G033
Pen Nibs stamp – A/F D028

Floral Fun – page 76
Penny's Vase stamp – A/F F020
Flower Accents stamp – A/F A046
Flower Head Border stamp – A/F E008
Double-sided Circles & Scrim stamp – A/F X003
Leaf Spray stamp – A/F D019
Double Vase stamp – A/F F011
Orchid Border stamp – A/F D015
Double-sided Grid Texture stamp – A/F X001

Keep in Touch – page 78
Post Script stamp – A/F G028
Treasured Memories stamp – A/F G032
Antique Dip Pens stamp – A/F G033 Pen
Nibs stamp – A/F D028
Triple Scalloped Tag stamp – A/F H013

Mosaic Magic – page 82
Orchid Border stamp – A/F D015
Palm Trees stamp – A/F D016
Palm Leaves stamp – A/F D017
Bubble Line stamp – A/F C031
Swirl Plaque stamp – A/F F002
Double-sided Stars & Swirls Texture stamp – A/F X002
Tiny Flower Accents stamp – A/F A046
Double-sided Circles & Scrim stamp – A/F X003

Holiday Memories – page 86
Wavy Lines stamp – A/F G012
Swirl Plaque stamp – A/F F002
Art Moulds – Letters S, E, A;
            – AM040 Fossil Snail

Shrunk in the Wash – page 90
Happy 18th Birthday stamp – A/F B041
Long-sleeved T-shirt stamp – A/F E030
Tie-top T-shirt stamp – A/F C039
Mini Skirt stamp – A/F D027
Frilled Mini Skirt stamp – A/F C037
Jeans stamp – A/F F023

Animal Magic – page 94
Sea Life Elements stamp – A/F G010
Double-sided Circles & Scrim stamp – A/F X003
Bubble Line stamp – A/F C031
Double-sided Crackle & Textured Paper stamp – A/F X005
Quilt Mosaic stamp – A/F G005
Dolly the Sheep stamp – A/F E015
Art Moulds – Butterfly AM131;
            – Elephant AM119

Precious Little Pages – page 96
Double-sided Abstract stamp – A/F X006
Pocket Watch stamp – A/F E031
Treasured Memories stamp – A/F G032
Secret Keys stamp – A/F G029

About the Author

Jane Pinder has been stamping for 13 years, since she bought her daughter, Samantha, a set of stamps for her 12th birthday. She runs her own stamping business in the Cotswolds, The Stamp Bug Ltd, where she retails and runs workshops. She also has an on-line shop, created and maintained by her son, Mike. She and her husband, Noel, manufacture the Artifacts range of stamps themselves.

Jane is Editor of *Craft Stamper* magazine (Traplet Publications), which started in the summer of 2000.

A life-long crafter, Jane has a particular passion for stamping, papercrafting, Dakota aeroplanes and Cliff Richard! Jane lives near Cirencester, Gloucestershire.

Acknowledgments

A special thanks to the team who worked on my book, including Jennifer Proverbs, Sarah Underhill, Bethany Dymond and Kelly Smith and a big thank you to Karl Adamson, the photographer, who was brilliant and with whom we had a lot of laughs.

To Vivienne Wells, commissioning editor, for persuading me to take this on and to my friend, Jane Greenoff, cross stitch guru, for suggesting me to Vivienne in the first place. You have a lot to answer for!

More thanks go to Penny Bearcroft and Ann March whose great help with the projects made this book possible. Without your assistance I would not have had enough hours in the day to complete the book. You both look after The Stamp Bug so well for me, which has enabled me to get on with the writing.

Thank you also to Anna Justice who has been a great friend and made some of the samples on the Gallery pages.

A huge thank you to my daughter, Sam and my son, Mike, for putting up with me being glued to the computer for days on end, even though I don't see you that often.

And finally a big thank you to my husband, Noel, who despite being an airline pilot and working strange hours, has done all the cooking and generally looked after everything, including me, while I worked!

Index